JEAN-CHARLES TREBBI

THE ART OF ORIGAMI BOOKS

ORIGAMI, KIRIGAMI, LABYRINTH, TUNNEL AND MINI BOOKS

BY ARTISTS FROM AROUND THE WORLD

 HOAKI

HOAKI

Hoaki Books, S.L.
C/ Ausiàs March, 128
08013 Barcelona, Spain
T. 0034 935 952 283
F. 0034 932 654 883
info@hoaki.com
www.hoaki.com

hoakibooks

The Art of Origami Books
Origami, Kirigami, Labyrinth, Tunnel and Mini Books by Artists from
Around the World

ISBN: 978-84-17656-85-0

© 2022 Hoaki Books, S.L.
First published by Editions Gallimard, Paris
© Editions Gallimard, collection Alternatives 2021
Original title: *L'art du livre Origami*

Author: Jean-Charles Trebbi
Translation: Kevin Alan Krell
Cover designer: spread

D.L.: B 10300-2022
Printed in China

• Coco Téxèdre.

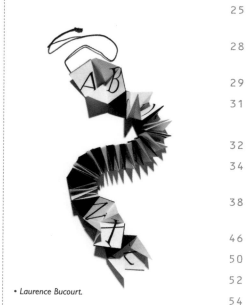

• Laurence Bucourt.

• Kevin Steele.

• Hedi Kyle.

• Jean-Charles Trebbi.

• Gérard Lo Monaco.

• Paul Johnson.

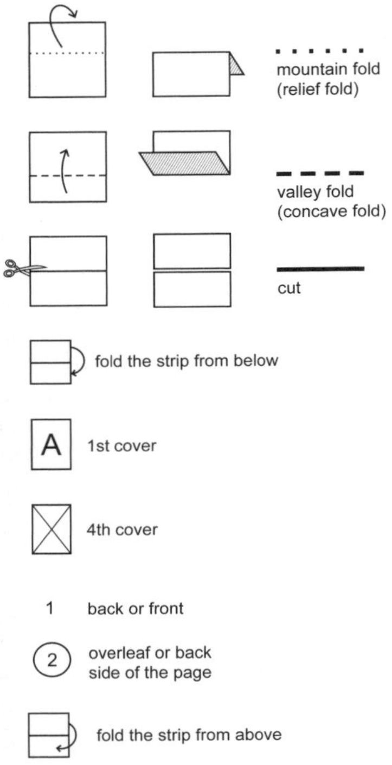

Astonishing books without binding

mountain fold
(relief fold)

valley fold
(concave fold)

cut

fold the strip from below

A 1st cover

4th cover

1 back or front

2 overleaf or back
side of the page

fold the strip from above

*• Symbols of graphic representation of folds
used in this book.*

While researching my previous books, *The Art of the Fold* and *The Art of Cutting*, I came across the extraordinary methods of certain artists who had created surprising, beautiful and efficient books. In addition to Masahiro Chatani, inventor of origami architecture and some of my own models, contemporary artists such as Bruno Munari, Katsumi Komagata, Ed Hutchins, Paul Johnson, Hedi Kyle, Werner Pfeiffer, Alisa Golden, Claire Van Vliet, Elizabeth Steiner and Joan Michaels Paque and artists from the world of origami such as Shuzo Fujimoto, Martin Wall, Paul Jackson and David Brill have invented extremely original books, often without any specific binding.

Yet, in the digital age, why would anybody want to create books without binding? Simply because the act of handling paper and giving it form is a concrete physical act, and because making these simple yet astonishing objects is a source of pleasure for children and adults.

For this reason, in this book I have compiled one hundred contemporary creations ranging from such diverse areas as artist and photography books to sales brochures, notebooks and travelogues. Through them, you will discover the folding and cutting techniques that made their creation possible: a repertoire of easy-to-make shapes and structures intended for artists and teachers as well as lovers of educational handicrafts, *scrapbooking* and creative entertainment. Here I am certain you will find useful tools to serve your imagination as I did. In these pages, you will also find thirty-five models that I created in this spirit, often using a single folded and cut sheet of paper, sometimes assembled with others but always unbound.

The traditional bases of the classic origami and kirigami folds (square or triangular preliminary base, lotus or diamond fold) are used in the models shown here. Frequently, however, these techniques have been adapted or reinvented according to the common principles of the art of origami, that is, the transfer from teacher to student and the sharing among origamists of all ages and levels. This generosity in the creative exchange makes the emergence of constantly renewing forms possible.

• *The Parallel of You, Gina Pisello, 2019*

"When the hands are busy, the spirit is at peace."
Akira Yoshizawa

Simple origami

• Paroles dissimulées, *Coco Téxèdre*, 2019.

Leporello

• *Kabuverdianu, Peter D. Gerakaris, 2021.*

• *L'ABC de l'aviateur, Isabelle Faivre, 2020.*
Folded, 5 x 8 x 2.5 cm (2 x 3 x1 in), unfolded,
70 cm (28 in).
"Leporello alphabet primer with double pages
in suede or leather sleeve. Print of old map
collages. Homage to aviation language and
airplane registrations through letters and words."
Marie-Christine Guyonnet., Librairie du Ciel.

A multifaceted accordion book

The *Hungarian map*, the *Turkish map*, the *twist fold* and the miura-ori are folds very familiar to origamists. When applied to books, they produce surprising results. The first of these folds is the leporello.

Also called "accordion book", "concertina book" or less frequently, "frieze book", leporello is the name of a book made with a single strip of paper whose pages are folded in a zig-zag pattern over each other like the bellows of an accordion.

This simple and practical format is the source of countless variations and experimentations, in addition to textbooks, brochures and artist books. During the Victorian Era in the United Kingdom, leporello books were often used as travel souvenirs.

There are three ways to handle a leporello book: you can open it like the pages of a codex, page by page and fold; read it with double pages like a traditional book; or unfold it completely to see the entire narrative and illustrations like a panorama book.

Original folds also allow for a variety of shapes and forms, especially when cuts are used that give the pages diminishing sizes. An unusual feature in one of Katsumi Komagata's books is that only half the image is shown in every other fold. As a result, different images are obtained depending on how the object is folded.

Many artists have used the leporello format in all sizes, from XXL to small concertinas that publishers such as Apeiron have made a specialty.

In the large-format category is *La Prose du Transsibérien* by Blaise Cendrars. Sophie Braun and Christian Caduc, responsible for the magnificent 2 meter-high (6.5 feet) reproduction published by Presses Universitaires de France, were awarded at the Nuit du Livre 2012 for their commendable work.

Another large-format example is the die-cut children's books published by Lirabelle. These books contain frescoes more than 2 meters (6.5 feet) long to appreciate the play of shadows. Examples include *Zèbres* by Anne Montbarbon and *Les musiciens de Brême* by Sébastien Orsini.

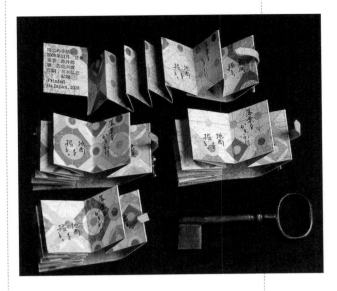

• The second letter, *Miyako Akai, 2008. Caligrafía de Minoru Sasaki. Impreso en resina tipográfica por Hiroshi Miki.*

• Les petites pensées, *Coco Téxèdre, 2001. Painted MBM paper cover, red cord, 15 x 10 cm (6 x 4 in). Leporello, Indian ink and acrylic on 250 g (92 lb) Vitela d'Arches with scarified markings and hidden writing, 20 x 67 cm (8 x 26 in). Unique copy.*

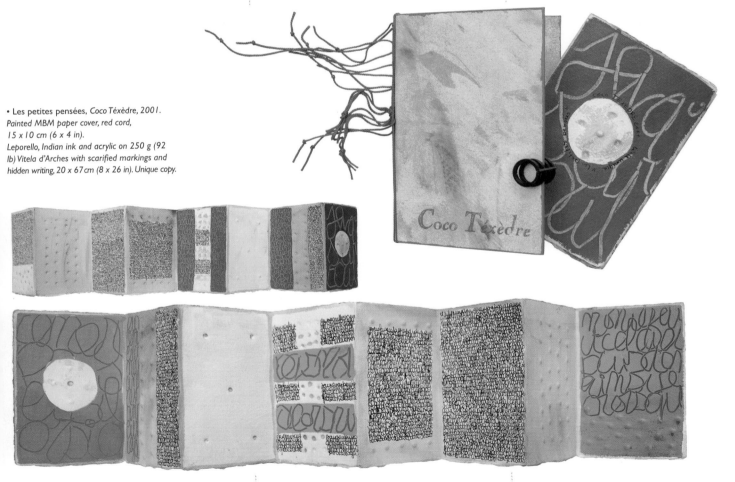

Hugo Pratt's Lignes d'Horizons is a unique creation, a large-format leporello designed by Éditions Courtes et Longues in association with the Musée des Confluences de Lyon in 2018. As if it were a long river, this beautiful work measuring 7 meters (23 ft) in length and printed on both sides contains a kind of dialogue between the private universe of Hugo Pratt and the collections of the museum.

Publisher Citadelles & Mazenod offers a spectacular accordion book by Xavier Barral i Altet and David Bates that reproduces the Bayeux tapestry at 46% of its original size, or 32.10 m by 27.5 cm (105 ft × 11 in) high, distributed in one hundred seven facets. Even more impressive is *Suite inexacte en homologie singulière* by Jean de Maximy, who over the course of forty years created this giant leporello illustrated with Rotring® and Indian ink. This fresco replete with embedded curves, a kind of hypnotic lunar landscape, is 38 meters (125 ft) long when unfolded. It was published in 2012 by Manufacture de L'image, in association with CNAP, Maison Rouge and the ABPi foundation.

Yet the most original leporello that I know is without a doubt *104 ans séparent nos voyages*, a remarkable creation extraordinarily documented by Frédérique Le Lous Delpech. Based on family archives, he created this marvelous panoramic book more than 50 meters (164 feet) long in which he used numerous animated book techniques.

Jean-Charles Trebbi, 2020.

• Hugo Pratt, Lignes d'Horizons, *éditions Courtes et Longues, Musée des Confluences, 2018.*

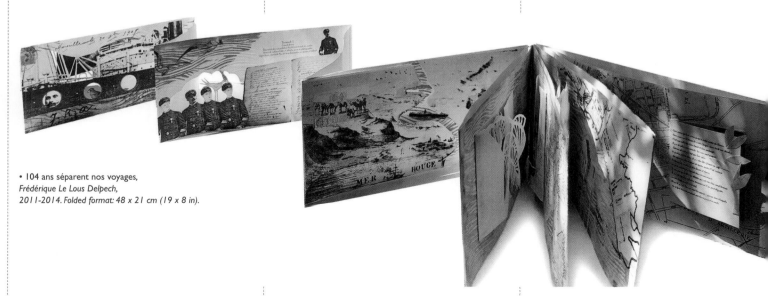

• 104 ans séparent nos voyages,
*Frédérique Le Lous Delpech,
2011-2014. Folded format: 48 x 21 cm (19 x 8 in).*

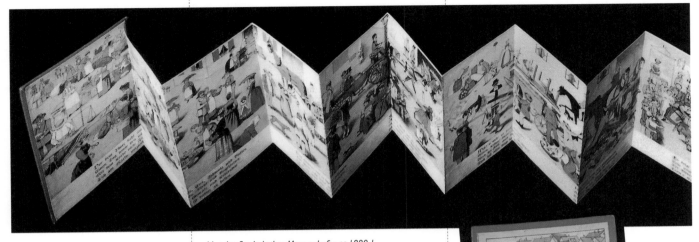

• Vor der Stadt, *Lothar Meggendorfer, ca. 1880. J.
Desse Collection.
Format: folded, 22 x 12 cm (9 x 5 in);
unfolded, 1.30 m (4.3 ft).*

Brief history of leporellos

JACQUES DESSE

In the history of books in the West, there are two main formats: rolled and folded. The first, the *volume*, is a long panorama that is unrolled. In the second, the *codex*, the sheet is folded and cut to form as many pages as needed. The codex transformed the way we read and use books. This ingenious invention of late antiquity conquered the world, starting in the 3RD and 4TH centuries. Its emergence was as significant an event at the time as the appearance of the computer was in the 20TH century. Another format, far less common, is found primarily in the Far East. Appearing mostly in Japan, the *"orihon"* consists of a single sheet of paper which is not rolled but folded and is uncut.

In the West, while there is some evidence between the 14th and 18th centuries, this format did not truly appear until the beginning of the 19th century, and not by accident: it was an unprecedented time of creativity and invention in art and in the book form. It was also a time when a new genre of the printed book appeared. Rather than being a compendium of knowledge, like a *bible,* this type of book was a playful and entertaining object without didactic purposes.

In fact, these *gadget works* were sold in *novelty shops*. And it was in this new and marginal sector of the publishing industry - that of image books, humorous books and travelogues - where this extraordinary format first appeared. One of the oldest examples that I know of in France is the second work by the great illustrator and caricaturist Gavarni, *Les Récréations diabolico-fantasmagoriques,* published in 1825.

Around the same time, a multitude of alphabet primers designed according to this model appeared. One of the most famous is the *Comic Alphabet* by Cruikshank, from 1836. All these types of books became very common, especially in the form of clothing and landscape collections.

Later, these books began to be called *leporellos* —after the name of Don Giovanni's servant who, in the opera by Mozart (1787)[1], presents a long list of his master's conquests on a concertina-fold sheet. More simply, they also began to be called *accordion books*, after the name of the musical instrument invented in 1829 in Austria. Less frequently, and more recently, we also come across the name "*frieze book*".

---

1. The word does not appear in the Littré dictionary or in the *Grand dictionnaire universel du XIXe siècle* by Larousse.

• La revue impériale, grand défilé des troupes de la garde et de la garnison de Paris devant l'empereur Napoléon III sur la Place du Carroussel, *Haguenthal, printer-editor, Pont-à-Mousson, ca. 1860. J. Desse Collection.*

• *Collection of original Japanese paintings (End of 19th century). Thick square leporello, orihon with pages folded and joined together. Format: folded, 11 x 10.5 x 3.5 cm (4 x 4 x 1 in); unfolded, approx. 4 m (13 ft); original ink drawings of different subjects: landscapes, flowers, animals, small sketches of people and houses. Nicolas Codron Collection.*

Certainly, the leporello is both an ordinary looking book, a folded paper parallelepiped with a traditional appearance, and a frieze or panorama that can be extended several meters and viewed as a whole like the ancient stories in images such as the Bayeux tapestry.

The creation of leporellos for young people continued in the 19th century, with such notable examples as the beautiful creations by the master of the genre Lothar Meggendorfer in the 1880s. Caricaturists, humorists and photographers did not ignore the format either.

It is well known that the publisher Père Castor published wonderful children's books such as the trilogy of panoramas by Russian avant-garde artist Alexandra Exter (1937-1938) and in the late 1940s, the friezes for coloring by Pierre Belvès. Designers in search of new forms delved deeper into this genre in the 1950s and

1960s. Among them was Enzo Mari and, most notably, Warja Lavater, an artist who starting in 1962, devoted her entire career to the creation of breathtaking abstract and narrative leporellos for children.

Painters seem to have become interested in this format belatedly. After the Japanist movement, Victor Segalen (*Stèles*, 1912) and Paul Claudel led the way, although their source of inspiration in adopting this form was not the European popular book but the noble tradition of the Far East. These timid beginnings quickly gave way to a dramatic moment in 1913, when *La Prose du Transsibérien*, the first "simultaneous book", appeared in Paris. Designed by Blaise Cendrars and Sonia Delaunay, this vertical leporello that mixes texts and images is one of the most beautiful and famous artist books of the 20th CENTURY. Also worth mentioning is *Repli* by Matisse and Rouveyre (1947) and the poem "*Liberté*" by Eluard illustrated by Fernand Léger in 1953. Later, in the early 1960s, this form became increasingly irresistible to artists. They used it almost invariably without text and transformed it into a multiple intermediary

between the image and the book, between icon and story. (Ruscha, *Every Building On Sunset Strip*, 1966; Fontana, *Concetto Spaziale*, 1966…).

Since then, interest in this format has continued to grow, becoming increasingly popular with artists and illustrators of children's books. If the magnificent *Anima* by Katy Couprie (1991) was an isolated case, the works by Kveta Pacovska were extremely influential, especially *Un Livre pour toi / Fold, Unfold*, published in 2004. Noteworthy among the many interesting books that have appeared in recent years are those by the Icinori duo, *Liberté* by Anouck Boisrobert and Louis Rigaud, and *Excentric city* by Béatrice Coron, which has the special quality of being completely die-cut, resulting in its play of shadows and transparency.

Today, leporellos incorporate new and daring combinations such as minuscule or gigantic books. They also embrace a third dimension, following the example of *Alphabeta Concertina*, a leporello in relief created by Ronald King in 1983.
Jacques Desse, May 2020.

- www.cleditions.com
- www.lirabelle.fr
- www.lanuitdulivre.com/livre/la-prose-du-transsiberien
- citadelles-mazenod.com/livres-exceptionnels/483-la-tapisserie-de-bayeux
- victorlejeune.com
- www.editionsapeiron.com
- www.bdgest.com/forum/leporello-t74917.html
- lamanufacturedelimage.com/project/jean-de-maximy-2
- www.origami-shop.com/images/Image/File/EBookMLucas/Pratique-du-pliage-M-Lucas.pdf
- chezleslibrairesassocies.blogspot.com

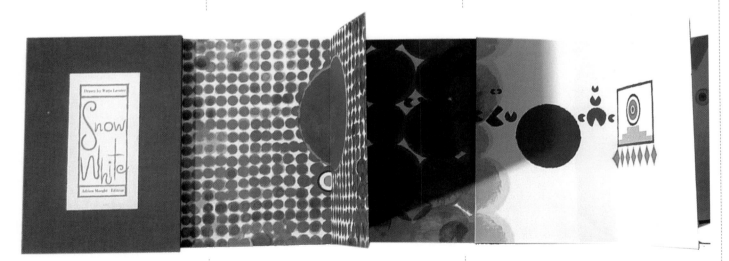

• Snow White, *Warja Lavater, Adrien Maeght, Paris, 1974. J. Desse Collection.*
Unfolded format: 16 x 11 x 4.56 m. (6 x 4 cm x 15 ft).

■ ORIGAMI BASE
SIMPLE FOLD

Coco Téxèdre

FRANCE

Corine, called Coco Téxèdre, is a plastic artist, painter and sculptor whose artist books defy classification. Irony and humor intertwine in her complex, often illegible writings that, paradoxically, evoke a cheerless world of pain, sadness and rebellion. Téxèdre works in her pleasant studio in the Seuilly hills, in Val de Loire, near the home of Rabelais, whose worlds have inspired fifteen of her books. Her creations appear in numerous public collections. "The artist book is fertile ground that combines the plastic image with the poetic in a single realm of experimentation where boundaries disappear, transgression is the norm and creation resists all labels. The artist becomes an architect in a publishing dystopia. Coco Téxèdre constructs a boundless semantic universe that incorporates the creation of books into an overall vision of art, a funereal space where paintings, sculptures and installations meet at the crossroads of a single work.

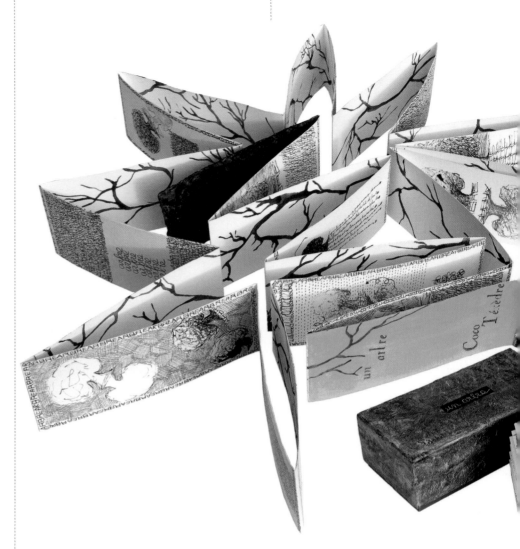

The multiple book is unique, singular and original, not bound by the yoke of mass production. The author possesses her textual space, sometimes pretextual, with shared complicity. Nearby, François Rabelais amuses himself, expanding and, once again, waging the incessant wars of Picrochole."
Text by Arnaud Schultz, 2020.

🖸 www.cocotexedre.com

• *Arbre...*, Coco Téxèdre, 2019.
Moulin de Pombié and leather cover Extract from Empreintes de l'arbre *by Suzanne Aurbach. Leporello, Indian ink and acrylic on 250 g (92 lb) Moulin du Gué® paper. Original drawings by Coco Téxèdre. Format: 16 x 118 cm (19 x 8 in).*
Unique copy

• Mélancolie d'un sentier qui s'efface,
Hélène Baumel, 2014.
Poems by Marcel Maillet, ten sugar-lift aquatints
by Hélène Baumel. Printed on 270 g/m² (100
lb) Canson Gravure, 10 copies. Presented in
Altuglas® sleeve.
Format: folded, 12.5 x 16.5 x 3 cm (5 x 6.5
x1 in); unfolded: 2.46 m (8 ft) or 1.60 m (5 ft)
fanned out.

Hélène Baumel

FRANCE

Hélène specializes in intaglio and wood engravings, in limited editions and artist books in collaboration with contemporary poets. She teaches wood and linoleum engraving at the Estampe de Chaville and has participated in numerous exhibitions in France and abroad since 1979. Among other distinctions, in 2018 she was awarded the Fondation Taylor M. et L. Navier prize. "I love all facets of nature, landscapes, mountains, water plains... I take the time to observe nature, retain what is essential and translate it later through different techniques: drawings, inking and engravings."
Text by Hélène Baumel, 2019.

✏ www.helenebaumel.com

• Dans les branches du temps, *Hélène Baumel, 2015.*
Poem by Marcel Maillet, ten linocuts by
Hélène Baumel. Printed on Japan paper and glued on
Kraft paper. Presented in a box with birch bark. 10
numbered copies.
Closed box: 22 x 31 x 2 cm (9 x 12 x 3 in).

• Laisser une trace, *Philippe Phérivong,*
2015. Leporello made of ten original ink and
acrylic creations. Bindings by Malica Lestang.
Binding covers made with a glued, frottage and
varnished paper technique.
Folded format: 12 x 12 cm (5 x 5 in).

Marjon Mudde
FRANCE

Marjon is a tireless, multifaceted artist
with an unquenchable thirst for research.
She likes to revisit old techniques and use
them, sometimes in unexpected ways, in
her engravings, artist books and ceramics.
She also does not hesitate to mix genres:
textile and ceramic in books, cardboard for
engravings, wood and metal in bookbinding.
Public and private institutions in France and
other countries regularly exhibit and collect
her creations. She teaches artist book
and engraving courses and workshops in
media libraries, museums and associations
throughout France.

✆ marjon-mudde.tumblr.com

✆ artmarjonmudde.wordpress.com

• Endymion, *Marjon Mudde, 2019.*
Materials: cloth, paper, leather and thread. Original
drawings. Éditions La Ville Haute. Format: folded, 22
x 17 x 7 cm (9 x 7 x 3 in); unfolded, 22 x 256 cm
(9 x 101 in).
Animated artist book made up of seven original
black drawings and seven watercolors.
Six of the seven white circles can be turned to reveal
the drawing, but the full moon in the middle is static.
Extract of a poem by Marguerite Yourcenar that
appeared in Mercure de France in 1929. In Greek
mythology, Endymion was the lover of the goddess
of the moon, Selene, who put him to perpetual sleep
so that she could admire his extraordinary beauty.
They had fifty children together, which represent
the interval of the fifty lunar months between the
Olympic Games.

■ RECTANGULAR BASE FOLDS AND TRIANGLE

• Triangle rectangle isosceles or half square base, rectangular strip made up of squares with a diagonal line reflected symmetrically like a snake.

• Wax super Betty, Isabelle Faivre, 2020. Triangular base lepoerello. African fabric and gouache. Unique piece in black sleeve. Format: folded 11 x 8 x 8 cm (4 x 3 x 3 in); unfolded, 70 cm (28 in).

🔖 meslivresinsolites.blogspot.fr

🔖 isabellefaivrepari.wixsite.com/artistepapier

■ HEXAGON BASE FOLD

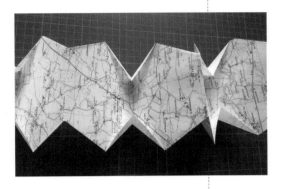

• Accordion-fold rectangular strip, with two V-shaped folds in the lower and upper part. Once the strip is folded, it is possible to cut different shapes, series of cutouts or stacked silhouettes, taking care not to cut the joining areas to the right and left (see the chapter Kirigami, pg. 62).

• Book of Non-Existent Animals - Bestiary or The Felt Book, Emile Goozairow, 2015. Book from the Alphabet ABC series. Collector's bestiary of non-existent animals, each corresponding to a letter in the English alphabet. The three-dimensional structure is foldable.

■ SPIRAL LEPORELLO

• Spiral book, Miyako Akai.
"I chose this structure to present the spiral visually. It's advantage lies in the fact that it's easy to prepare repeatedly, but it has one drawback: it's difficult to turn over. As for the characteristics of the paper, I chose a thick paper that doesn't tear and opens like a spring when unfolded. I attached magnets to both covers to close them."
Miyako Akai, December 2019.

"Spiral"

Repeat mountain folds and valley folds.

front cover

folded paper = text block

back cover

• Original design by Miyako Akai.

■ TURKISH MAP SQUARE BASE SECTION AND STRIP

The *Turkish map fold* is similar to the design created by Anders Oswald Palm, who patented it in 1947. It is a well-known fold in origami, called a *"waterbomb base"*, that begins with a square sheet format. Later, we will see another base with reverse folds called a "preliminary base" which serves as the beginning of many origami models.

This type of fold is also called an *"explosion card"* or *"explosion fold"*, since when opening the page, the shape of the fold forces the paper to unfold like a *pop-up*.
A version is the *Hungarian map fold*, sometimes called a *"diamond fold"* or *"lotus book fold"*, with a simple difference in the folds:

— in the *Turkish map*, the base is the *waterbomb* fold made from two mountain fold diagonals and half of a valley fold (sector that joins the centers of the two opposite sides);

— in the *Hungarian map*, the base is the preliminary base fold made up of two half valley folds and one diagonal mountain fold (segment that joins the opposite angles).

These two folds are often confused, and it is not uncommon to find videos on the web that use the terms mistakenly.

Many types of folds are possible:
— square 20 x 20 cm (8 x 8 in) format.
— A4 or A3 rectangular format.
— A4 format but with diagonals centered and offset toward the center of the sheet;
— circular format.

• Das Goldene Ei, *Emile Goozairow, 2015. A version of the old Russian tale* Ryaba Kurochka *in which the adventure begins with a magical egg.*

Here we have two methods of execution to choose from:
— copy the drawing of the model and mark the mountain and valley folds;
— analyze the form of the fold and reproduce the sequence of folds.
This last method tends to be more interesting, as it allows for the discovery of variations through the handling of the paper.

Gina Pisello

UNITED STATES

Gina Pisello glorifies paper in astounding creations that, while based on simple forms, often require mathematical calculations such as her studies of spirals.

"I've played with paper most of my life. First, when I was a little girl, I folded simple flowers; later, as an adult, I learned to make artist books. Recently, I've also begun to make sculptures. I'm fascinated by lines, shadows and textures. I force myself to transform my fetish material into dynamic three-dimensional sculptures that invite the viewer to enter and find hidden depth and meaning. I explore themes of time (on a personal and geologic level) and nature in all its exquisiteness.

It made sense to me to use a fold in the maps because I'd made travel books such as *The Road to Spring* and *Companion Star*.

One of the advantages of Turkish and Hungarian map folds is that they're small when they're closed but open easily to reveal a larger format.

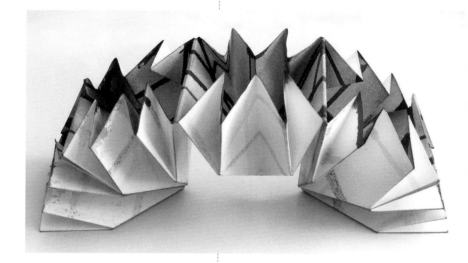

• The Road to Spring, *Gina Pisello, 2015.*

As a printing technique, I chose color spray ink for the deep blue of *Companion Star* and the same inks (Tim Holtz Distress Inks) for the colors of spring in *The Road to Spring*. To make the lines of the map, I poured ink onto a large sheet, a technique I learned from Jill Berry. I wrote the text of each book by hand and purposely divided *The Road to Spring* into several stages, following our spring journeys between New York and Alabama to visit family. Unlike many of my works, these two books are autobiographical."
Gina Pisello, February 2020.

✆ www.ginapisello.com

• Companion Star, *Gina Pisello, 2015.*

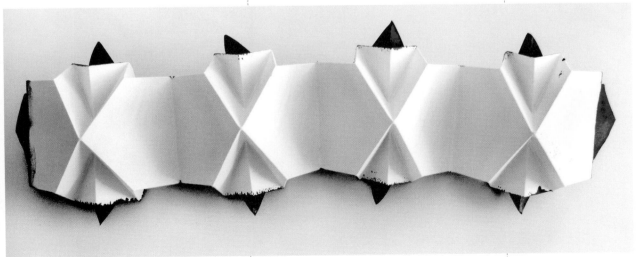

■ TURKISH MAP
RECTANGULAR BASE BREVET PALM

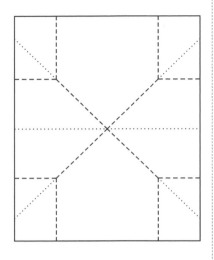

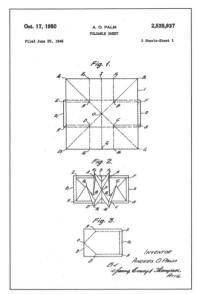

• *Brevet Palm. Fold on an initially square or rectangular format. It is possible to experiment with variations, lengthening more or less the diagonals in the center.*

• *Carousel of Miracles, Emile Goozairow, 2015. Based on one of his large engravings, Carousel of Miracles, Emile composed a text and created a book that, when opened, transforms into a windmill. It can also be called "paper flower". Another version of this work consists of a single image that can be gathered in a booklet.*

■ TURKISH MAP CIRCULAR BASE
DOUBLE FOLD, OVERFLOW
AND STRIP

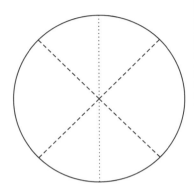

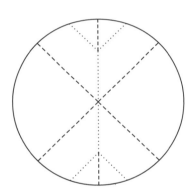

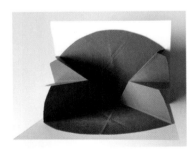

• *The model is made up of Turkish map-fold modules, applied here to a circle base. It can be enriched by adding additional folds, as well as overflowing forms. Some modules can also be inserted in a leporello base.*

Eni Looka

FRANCE

Eni is a book illustrator, graphic designer and artist known for his magnificent postal art creations, for which he makes his own stamps, often with an abundance of humor. Here we have a travelogue with a circle base.

"I like going on trips. I like drawings.... I like travelogues. And I like handmade books, pop-ups.
A long time ago, I wanted to create a folding booklet according to the 'quarter of a circle, three folds' principle". So I constructed this mini story in eleven images (watercolors and paper cutouts), a summary of my beautiful journeys to Thailand."
Text by Eni Looka, July 2020.

✍ unevieunarbre.wordpress.com/festival-dart-postal-2020/%E2%96%88-eni-looka

✍ www.amazon.fr/Eni-Looka-fait-ses-timbres

• *Thaïlande, Eni Looka, 2020.*
Folded format: 10 x 10 x 2.5 cm (9 x 12 x 3 in).

■ TURKISH MAP
DIMINISHING CIRCLE BASE

STEAMpop

AUSTRALIA

"Miura folds offer numerous possibilities for traditional and experimental books. The right borders of a certain number of folds of uniform size stack up and align to form a traditional book structure with two covers. The work assumes a twisted appearance as the number of folds increases. The change in alignment and size results in different shapes."

Within the framework of her artistic activity, Lisa Giles has been creating origami structures for more than ten years, ever since she studied the influence of the fold on the design of artist books while completing her master's degree. Like almost everybody, Lisa began by folding square sheets, but her fascination with curves stimulated her curiosity. Circular paper structures, in addition to providing clean and straight lines, present marvelous curves that offer different aesthetic variations.

Lisa associated herself with art and design professors Annette Mauer and Melissa Silk, of STEAMpop, who lead workshops that combine mathematics and the art of folding. STEAMpop proposed transforming the learning of geometry into an artistic practice. Currently, she collaborates on the *circulus project*. Navigating between craftwork and computerized production enables building precise sculptural forms without sacrificing the integrity of the simple Miura fold.

The Miura fold is considered a *shape memory origami*. Its mechanical behavior depends on the memory properties of the material such that after unfolding the sheet of paper, it is easy to refold it and for the paper to recover its compact form. This folding method enables opening and closing the paper in one swift movement, as if it were a map.

Origami theorists say this method offers more creative freedom. The *pop out*, also called *Turkish map fold* , made from a square or rectangular map, has also adopted the Miura fold.

Taken from comments by Lisa Giles, Annette Mauer and Melissa Silk, February 2020.

✎ Lisa Giles, paper artist: www.lisagiles.com.au/

✎ Annette Mauer and Melissa Silk - STEAMpop: www.steampop.zone

✎ Miura circular fold: *A Synthesis of Sectors from Bridges Math Art conference*, 2019. archive.bridgesmathart.org/2019/bridges2019-605.pdf

• *The decreasing diameter of the Miura folds results in a spinning recurring modular structure that recalls Jurassic and Cretaceous ammonites.*

• The Miura fold, which retains the simple flexibility of the Turkish map fold, has improved thanks to diminishing repetition of the folded circles. When this combination is applied to the rules of modular origami, the result is sculptures that suggest exponential growth and the marvels of biomimetics.

• Circular creations by Lisa.

■ TWIST FOLD, SHUZO FUJIMOTO MODEL ON SQUARE BASE

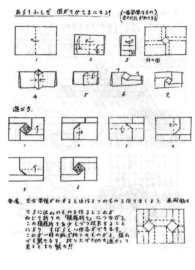

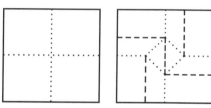

• It is generally accepted that Shuzo Fujimoto, (Osaka, 1922-2015), a Japanese origamist known throughout the world, is the creator of this specific model, which he published in 1976 in his book 3D Origami with Noriko Fujimura as co-author.
This fold is used frequently in the art of origami, especially to make tessellations, a technique that consists of folding the sheet of paper onto itself forming repeating geometric patterns. According to David Lister, eminent origami specialist with the BOS (British Origami Society), this twist technique was discovered at the same time, apparently, by another origami master, Yoshihide Momotani, who used it in his first books on folded flowers.

■ VARIATIONS OF RECTANGULAR BASE TWIST FOLD

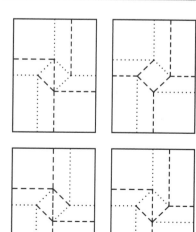

• Twist variations, J.-Ch. Trebbi, 2017.
Folded format: 10 x 2 cm (4 x 0.8 in).
"I imagined these models by experimenting with and reversing folds in a simple way.
Based on the same twist-base plan, different patterns emerged. It involves a play of folds around the twist in which graphic symbols from one to ten are presented. Certain symbols are only visible when the fold is opened. Here, the twist pattern is on a rectangular base, but a square base or one of other shapes is also possible."

Jean-Jacques Delalandre

FRANCE

A folding enthusiast since 1963, Jean-Jacques Delalandre is honorary president of the MFPP, a French paper folding movement, and creator of the association PliÁrt. Since 1989, he has managed a database that contains references to more than 3,000 books and 45,000 models with information about their origin and author.

"In its strictest form, an origami booklet consists of a single folded sheet of paper that forms both the pages and the cover, without cutting or gluing. However, in less purist versions, the sensible use of cuts enables, for example, obtaining more pages. Some models have several sheets to increase the amount of interior pages or to create the cover.

The creation of an origami booklet presents various difficulties. These lie both in coordinating the making of the cover with the colors on the right side and back of the sheet and managing the shift of the pages due to the numerous thicknesses of the paper; the heavier the paper the more pronounced this effect will be. This final model rarely contains more than eight pages if a single sheet is used. Some designs have more pages thanks to the use of several sheets of paper, whether folded or cut.

The initial sheet tends to have a square base of 15 x 15 cm (6 x 6 in) or 20 x 20 cm (8 x 8 in). Some models have an A4 (U.S. letter) or A3 (tabloid) rectangular base. It is therefore crucial to choose sheets that do not exceed 70 g/m² (26 lbs).

Various origami mini book models by Jean-Jacques Delalandre.

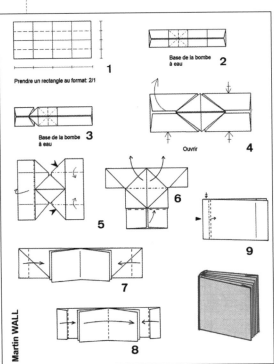

Prendre un rectangle au format: 2/1

1

Base de la bombe à eau **2**

Base de la bombe à eau **3**

Ouvrir **4**

5

6

7

8

9

Martin WALL

• *Original model by Martin Wall, English origamist, member of the BOS (British Origami Society), taken from the magazine Le Pli no. 51, Summer 1992. Made from a single folded sheet, this model could be titled "onbox", since it has the special feature of being able to transform into a box. With 15 x 15 cm (6 x 6 in) format, a mini book of 2.8 x 2.8 cm (1.1 x 1.1 in) is obtained. The use of very thin paper is essential, as the amount of folds creates thickness.*
In the chapter devoted to Kirigami, the book created by Jeroen Hillhorst from two sheets and the card holder books by Humiako Huzita, as well as some variations, are shown (see pg. 59).

✆ www.britishorigami.info

One of the simplest models is made with a long rectangle folded in two unequal parts. The excess of the wider part is folded over the narrower part to form a tube. The resulting strip is then folded and, finally, the last page is fit into the first.

Models for advanced folders are characterized by the following: optimizing the number of pages, minimizing as much as possible the shift factor due to the thicknesses of the paper, ensuring the cover is clearly larger than the pages to enhance the aesthetic effect, and, of course, taking advantage of the colors on the right side and back of the sheet. These models entail many folding stages and require the use of light-weight paper with good tear resistance.

Kraft paper is a good material. I like to use parchment paper like the kind used in the kitchen that comes in rolls. Thin yet resistant, it allows for a significant increase in the number of pages. Thanks to it, I was able to create a 1 cm × 2 cm (0.4 × 0.8 in) booklet for a theater piece. An actor removed a one-meter (3 ft) long ribbon with a message written on it. The silk paper used in sewing also has many advantages: it is even lighter, 40 to 60 g/m² (15 to 22 lb), it is resistant and comes in 1.20 m (4 ft) rolls.

The creations of David Brill, Kunihiko Kasahara and Yoshihide Momotani are good examples.

Other very interesting models associate books with other objects.

The best example is the 'heart book' by Francis M.Y. Ow, which appears in her book *Origami Heart*, published in 1989 and available online (www.owrigami.com)."
Jean-Jacques Delalandre, May 2020.

✎ MFPP, French Movement for Paper Folders, French association that promotes origami: mfpp-origami.fr/

✎ Origami base models posted on the Internet by J.-J. Delalandre: origami.jubile.fr/

✎ For anyone who wants to learn about origami book folding, *The New World by Kunihiko Kasahara*, published in 1989 by Sanrio, is a good reference where you can find various models by different origamists.

• Little red book fold, *Jean-Jacques Delalandre*
There are two different ways to indicate the operations or sequences of folds needed to make an origami model:
the diagram and the fold pattern.
"The diagram is to origami what the score is to music, that is, a graphic representation that allows the folder to create an origami object. A diagram consists of a series of drawings along with different symbols that indicate the operations to perform to obtain the final model. These symbols represent what is called the solfeggio of paper folders, which is the same in all countries." Guillaume Denis, Origami, vol. 1, les Bases, ed. Eyrolles, 2018.
On the back, a crease pattern or CP is the pattern obtained from valley and mountain folds after making and unfolding the model. It is worth mentioning that the patterns can be used in some cases to validate the authorship of a model.

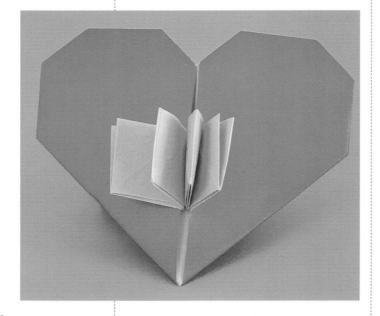

• Heart book, *Francis M.Y. Ow, 1989.*

• Red line: mountain fold, blue line: valley fold.

■ FLAT MIURA-ORI FOLD

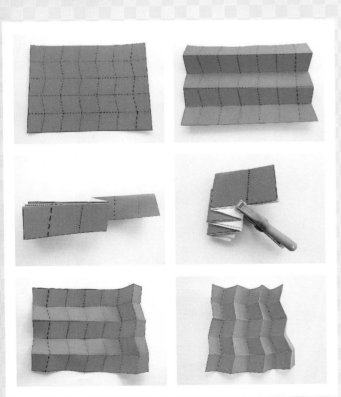

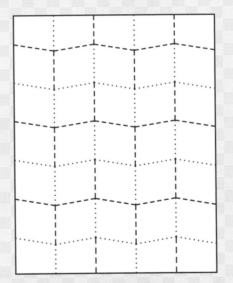

• This very particular type of fold bears the name of its inventor, Japanese astrophysicist Koryo Miura. Assembled in the 1970s, it is a kind of lengthwise accordion fold yet with a slight angle of inclination set crosswise. This angle facilitates easy and quick unfolding. Koyo Miura had the idea for this fold when he was studying aerospace structures at the Institute of Space and Aeronautical Science, Tokyo University.

NASA has used this fold in research on solar sails in space, but there are many other examples of its use both in scientific areas and tourist maps.

It is a herringbone pattern, made up of a grid whose sides are parallelograms. To unfold it, all you have to do is pull on the two diagonal points and fold back holding the map by the diagonal ends and closing it toward the center.

The Miura-ori fold has been the focus of numerous studies. It has given rise to many variations due to the large community of origamists throughout the world that includes researchers in the practical application of science. An example of a possible variation consists of making a herringbone fold for every two folds, resulting in a decreasing fold, while the alternating change of fold angle defines a curved fold.

modular
origami

• Origami Window, *Peter D. Gerakaris, 2021.*

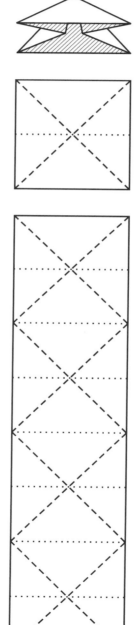

The term modular origami *means
that various elements, identical
or not, are folded separately and
later assembled for the purpose of
making a model.*
There are two possible techniques:
*assembly of modules and folding
repeating modules, arranged side
by side or on a strip.*

• *In origami terminology, this fold made on a
square base is called a waterbomb. The folds
are reversed: the mountain folds become valleys
and the valley folds mountains. In this way, a
preliminary base is easily created that serves as
a starting point for different models.*

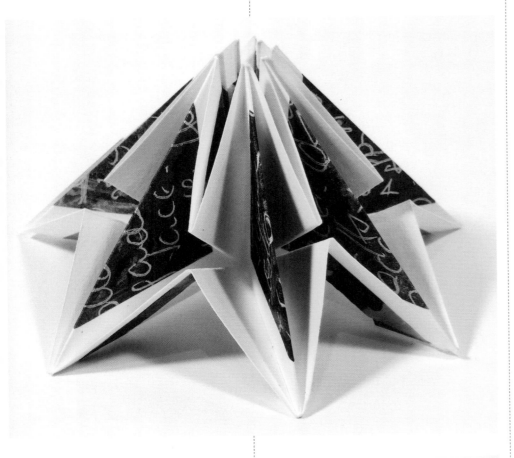

Annwyn Dean
GREAT BRITAIN

Annwyn is an embroiderer, creator of books and engraver. She lives and works in the United Kingdom, in Yorkshire.

Her books are inspired by fragments of old textile materials that she collected over the years while teaching embroidery. Each page she creates is enriched by the complex stories that these fragments of textile fabrics tell about their creators, owners and their comings and goings across the world and through the centuries.

When handled, the book allows for a connection between the artist and the viewer, establishing a link with the history of the fabric itself.

Her books are made through collography printing.

Annwyn's creations form part of the collections of the V&A museum, the Tate Library and universities in the United Kingdom and the United States, as well as different private collections.

🖙 annwyndean.co.uk

🖙 annwyndean.co.uk/blog

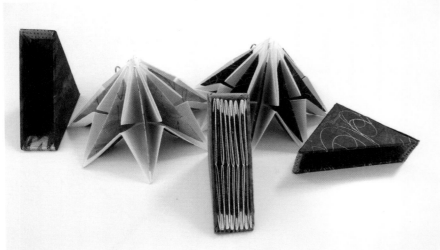

• Untitled, *Annwyn Dean*, 2017.
Three 8 cm (3 in) high copies

Frédérique Le Lous Delpech

FRANCE

"Often my books are single pieces. In any case, they seldom exceed ten copies. In their creation, time acts as a necessary breath. A pause. A stop in the image. I show infinite gratitude to the paper. And I like that it is handmade. The plate, previously engraved, is joined lovingly to the paper under a copper-plate engraving press. When the paper is printed, it expresses through my images a daily event, an instant, an emotion, an immobile journey. A book made by hand from start to finish can only be a unique object."

✎ www.atelierdespetitspapiers.com

• L'Abécédaire rare et précieux, *Text and illustrations by Frédérique Le Lous Delpech; folds, Jean-Charles Trebbi, 2010.*
Showcase with thirty-six boxes, print drawer style in four sections in two separable components. A bestiary with twenty-six animals, from A to Z based on the Dictionnaire des mots rares et précieux (ed. 10/18, 1996).

■ *WATERBOMB BASE*
TRIANGLE BASE

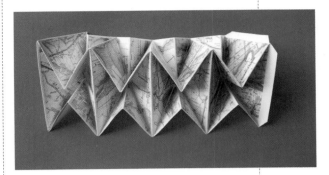

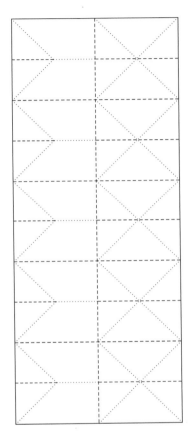

• This unique and magical model forms a corolla that has the special feature of being reversible. It is made with a strip of waterbomb modules to which semi-modules are added in the upper part.

The drawing represents a strip of five modules. To create the corolla, eight modules are needed. After preparing the assembly of folds, a small linking strip is added to close the model. Holding the corolla in both hands, rotating the assembly from the outside to the empty interior of the corolla results in a new arrangement of figures similar to a flexagon.

(Creation of J.-C. Trebbi, 2019.)

DIAMOND FOLD:
PRELIMINARY BASE
OR SQUARE BASE
MODULE AND STRIP

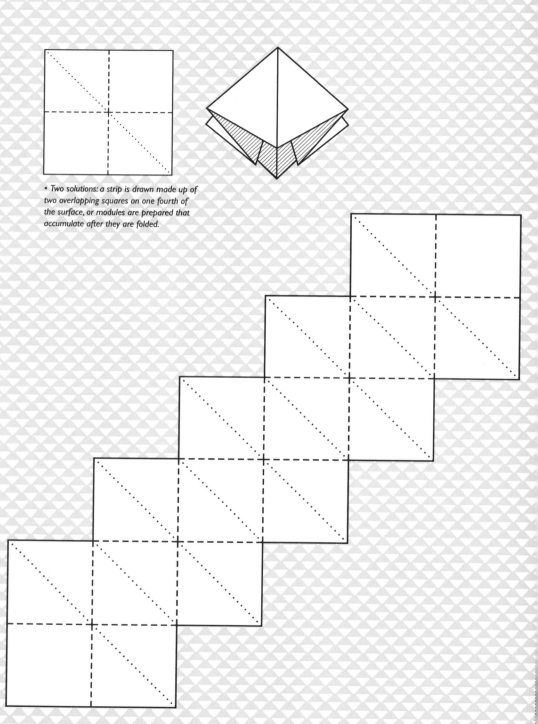

• *Two solutions: a strip is drawn made up of two overlapping squares on one fourth of the surface, or modules are prepared that accumulate after they are folded.*

■ PRELIMINARY BASE
REVERSE FOLDS

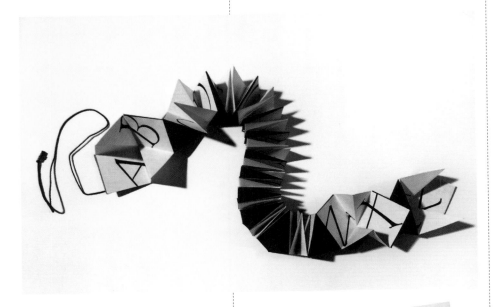

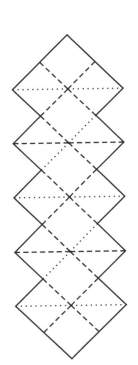

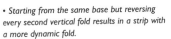

• *Starting from the same base but reversing every second vertical fold results in a strip with a more dynamic fold.*

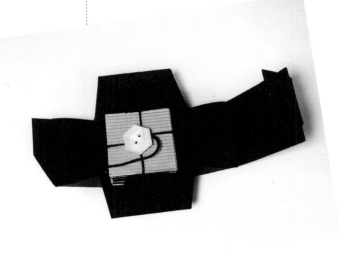

• Romaines, *alphabet primer, origami fold pages. Format: folded, 4.5 x 4.5 x 3 cm (5 x 6.5 x1 in); unfolded: 6 x 6 x approx. 120 cm (2 x 2 x approx. 47 in). Pages: elephant-skin paper 110 g/m² (41 lb), black and ivory. Cover: micro fluted, cord and mother-of-pearl button*

Laurence Bucourt
FRANCE

"The starting point of the project is the book form, made of pages with an origami preliminary base fold. I want to create a contrast between the form (the broken pages) that makes reading difficult and the background (Roman capitals) with a classic and smooth appearance. I decided to paint large letters emerging from the canvas of the sheet to create dynamics and establish a dialogue between the letters and the paper. The elephant-skin paper, whose color and appearance recall the texture of stone, reminds me of letters etched onto Roman monuments.

This book consists of twenty-five folded pages. The letters (two per page) are painted on thirteen ivory-colored pages. These alternate with twelve black-colored pages that serve as hinges glued to the back.
The letters are painted with a black velvet gouache brush. The cover is a brown micro-fluted square glued on the binding. A sewn button on the front cover and a string are used to close the book.

The structure is easy to construct and assemble. It has a pop-up effect and unfolds like a wreath. However, the creases remain pronounced and the book cannot be placed flat. For that reason, the book is not very legible."
Laurence Bucourt, 2019.

🖰 laurencebucourt.com

Kevin Steele

UNITED STATES

Kevin Steele is a graphic designer and book designer. He lives in Atlanta, Georgia. His professional activity focuses mostly on the creation of trademarks, visual identities and publications. His personal research focuses on movable books and paper engineering. He is interested in the ways structure, movement and interaction can improve visual communication. Kevin's creations, some of which are included in different collections, has been exhibited and published all over the world.

He is a member of AIGA and The Movable Book Society (United States association of animated book enthusiasts). In 2014, he was a finalist for the prestigious Meggendorfer prize.

"*Naughty but Nice* is an irreverent book in which recommendations related to social etiquette are contrasted with provocative illustrations. The text was taken from etiquette manuals published from 1847 to 1950. The images are from illustrated novels from the same period.

The tulip-fold structure is a response to the double-side format of the content: the polite text is on one side and the naughty images are on the other.

It seemed important to me that it was a miniature work. It had to be quite intimate and small to fit in a lover's pocket, almost like a seduction manual. The velvet cover and soft and carnal colors inside produce a sensation of sensuality and romance. Each page can be viewed separately, but the book can also be opened entirely and read all at once."

Kevin Steele, 2020.

✉ movablebooksociety.org

✉ mrkevinsteele.com

Gentlemen, before putting your arm around a lady's waist, you should explain to her that it is your intention to dance.

When you call on a girl, leave at 10:30 o'clock or earlier. When you are going, leave without a prolonged leave-taking.

• Naughty but Nice, *Kevin Steele, 2010.*
Folded book: 3.75 x 3.75 x 1.25 cm (1.5 x 1.5 x 0.5 in); unfolded: 40 x 10 x 0.62 cm (16 x 4 x 0.2 in). 90 copies.
Miniature book, recto-verso tulip fold, letterpress printed on French Mod-Tone paper with two-tone patterns on two sides with photopolymer plates.
Laval silkscreen print velvet covers, embossed and glued with decorative paper.

Diana Bloomfield

UNITED STATES

Diana Bloomfield is a world-renowned photographer specializing in 19TH century photographic printing techniques, in particular, processes based on gum biochromate, platinum and cyanotype prints. She currently lives in Raleigh, North Carolina.

"I love to think of books as sculptures: tactile, three-dimensional and intimate. For this reason, I began to create these handmade artist books, in single copies, in which I include details of my biochromate and cyanotype prints They collect images from the series *"The Old Garden"*, made with 19th century printing techniques. I believe the manual quality of these images and the garden theme harmonize wonderfully. Now that I've made a print run, I can't wait to fold, sew and bind and give it another form and a new life."
Diana Bloomfield, February 2020.

✎ dhbloomfield.com

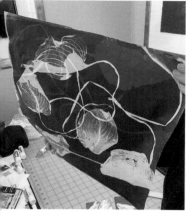

• Gossamer Wings, *Diana H. Bloomfield, 2019.*
Origami accordion book Format: folded, 6.25 x
6.25 cm (1.5 x 1.5 in); unfolded, 52.5 cm (21 in).
Hand-brushed with cyanotype emulsion on Gampi
Japanese paper, it is a still image of butterfly and
dragonfly wings. The center origami fold is glued to
each end, on the front and back, with a 6 cm (2.4
in) piece of cardboard, also covered with still images
brushed with cyanotype and printed on Gampi
Japanese paper. The Gampi paper not only accepts
a brushed emulsion well but also can be opened and
folded easily when the book is flat. The thinness of this
paper required a relatively small fold, since the bigger
it is the more of the structure is lost when opening
the book.

• The making of an origami dragon book by
Diana H. Bloomfield.
The origami accordion book is also called a
"serpent book" or "origami dragon book".
The name of this book is somewhat misleading,
since a single sheet of paper is used in a
genuine origami fold while this book uses five.
Still, it corresponds to the idea of origami insofar
as it uses square paper sheets and transforms
them into a sculpture.

Peter D. Gerakaris

UNITED STATES

Peter D. Gerakaris is an American multidisciplinary artist whose paintings, installations and kaleidoscopic sculptures address such themes as the dichotomy between nature and culture. His works are exhibited in different permanent institutional collections.

The artist's hybrid focus, nurtured by myriad international influences, music, iconography and perspectives, evokes the process of globalization that unfolds nearly as savagely and chaotically as nature itself. This multidisciplinary focus includes a wide variety of subject matter explored in painting, works on paper, murals, installations and origami sculpture.

Characterized by kaleidoscopic motifs and a tropical color palette, Gerakaris' meticulously superimposed details invite viewers to explore actual worlds inside other worlds. Privileging unconventional formats such as *tondo* (circular canvas), origami forms and alveolar structures, Gerakaris' work is simultaneously macro- and microscopic in nature, transporting observers through a metaphysical dream window.

"I think of these works as sculptural models for large pavilions that I hope to build one day. We could call them book sculptures. In general, I use two formats: origami and accordion."

Peter D. Gerakaris, January 2020.

✇ **www.petergerakaris.com**

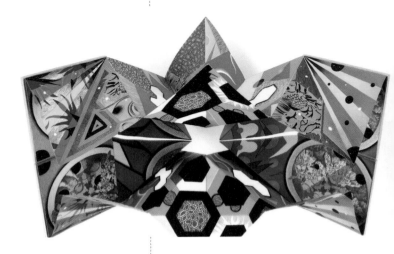

• Cosmicarium Origami, *Peter D. Gerakaris, 2021.*
Mixed technique on paper and wood.
Folded format: 76 x 30 x 30 cm (9 x 12 x 3 in).
Private collection (Shaker Heights, Ohio).

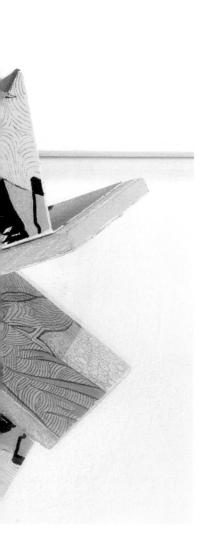

• Pandora's Box, *Peter D. Gerakaris, 2021.*
Folded format: approx. 66 x 20.5 x 15.5 cm.
(26 x 8 x 6 in).
Origami sculpture for the 2019 Mykonos
Biennial (Apathia). Gouache, acrylic, Mylar
mirror and yupo paper with figures painted
on a mirror box.
Mykonos Biennial Collection.

• Garden of Aquatic Delights I,
Peter D. Gerakaris, 2021. Accordion book (seen
with closed cover), mixed techniques on paper
and wood.
Format: folded, 50 x 25 x 25 cm (20 x 10 x 10 in).
William Lim Living Collection (Hong Kong, CH).

■ TRIANGULAR BOOK WITH STRIPS

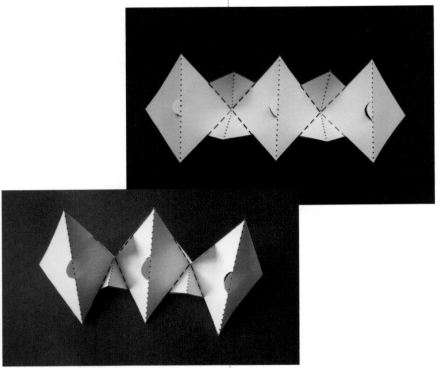

■ SPIRAL BOOK
HEXAGON PAGES

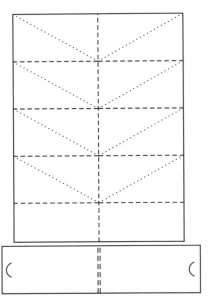

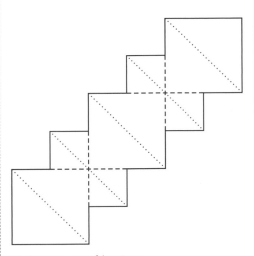

• In this version, some of the strips are eliminated to allow for the creation of a triangular-shaped book when folded. In the example, the semicircles we see in the strips indicate the possibility of creating elements in relief.

• It reproduces the proportions of the drawing of the five double strips. Make the mountain and valley folds to obtain this book with a hexagonal shape when folded. The cover has two notches that fit together to close the book.
(Creation of J.-C. Trebbi, 2019.)

Gina Pisello

UNITED STATES

"I love to play with paper. I also like to invent new structures and then extend and shrink them or change the folding pattern. The squares that form the base of this structure change in size, going from 10 cm (4 in) to 5 cm (2 in). This composition of *Spiral Atlas* is based on Turkish map folds that include Hungarian folds in the middle of each section."
Gina Pisello, February 2020.

✎ www.ginapisello.com

• Spiral Atlas, 2016.
Folded format: 12.5 cm x 8.75 x 6.25 cm (5 x 3 x 2 in).

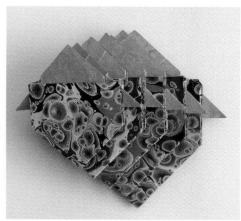

• Mini Spiral Atlas, *Gina Pisello, 2016.*
Folded format: *5 x 3.75 x 3.15 cm (9 x 12 x 3 in).*
Juxtaposition of different folds and diminishing spirals.

■ HUNGARIAN FOLD
HUNGARIAN MAP FOLD
"X" FOLD

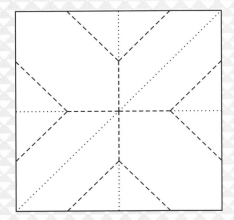

• *Tourist map of Stockholm, Stockholms Enskilda Bank advertising material.*

• What is the difference between the Hungarian map fold and the *preliminary base?* *The preliminary base functions as a starting fold. After it is made, it suffices to fold the open side mountains toward the center - as shown - to obtain a rhomboid shape.*
In the drawing, the angles of the square have been cut, resulting in an interesting shape.

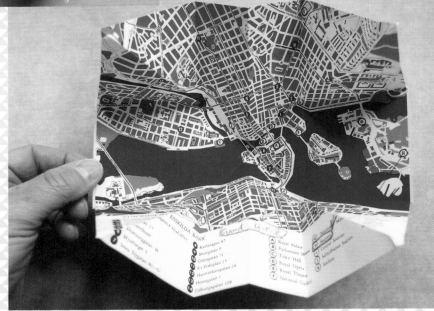

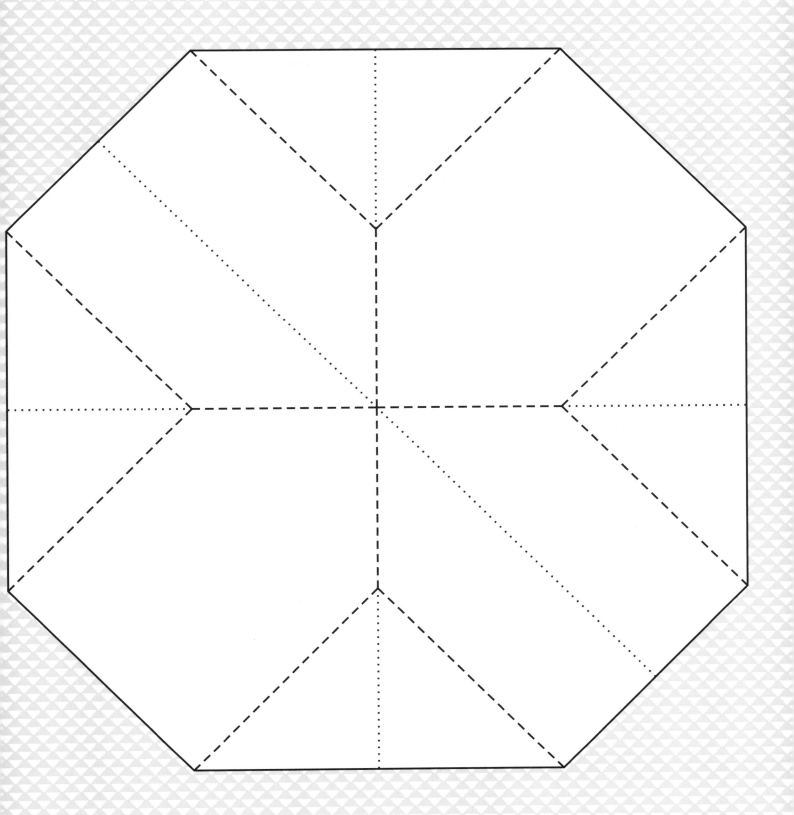

■ HEART FOLD MODULE AND ASSEMBLY

• Module cœur, Jean-Charles Trebbi, 2019.
After folding the modules, the model is
assembled with paper triangles folded in two, fit
together sideways.
The structure can be made with triangles facing
toward the bottom or top.

■ PETAL MODULE AND REGROUPING

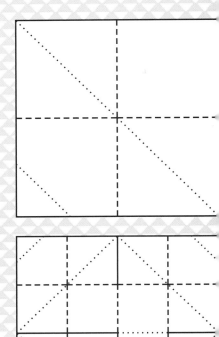

• Based on the assembly of four Hungarian
modules, cut or made with a single sheet with
incisions, a book with four pages that unfold
individually is obtained..

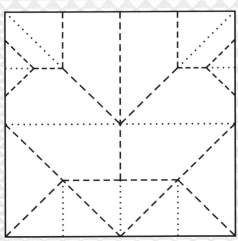

  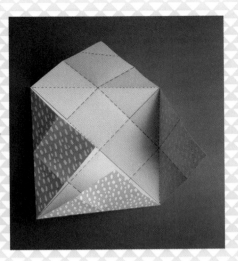

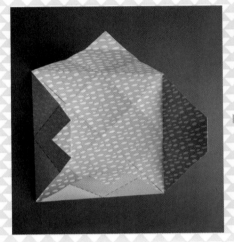 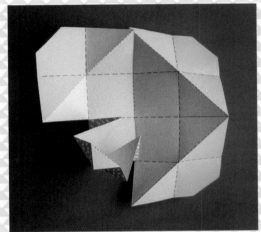 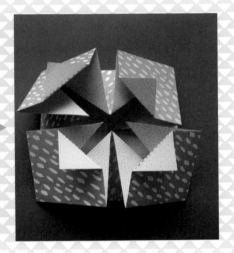

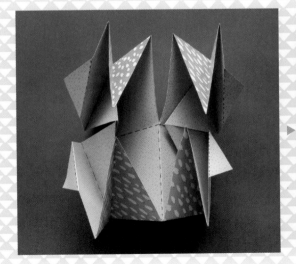  

The traditional art of Zhen Xian Bao

CHINA

The structure of the Chinese popular art of Zhen Xian Bao (or Shu Bao) is unusual and still relatively unknown.

In fact, it is not a book but a kind of sewing case used by the Miao, Dong and Yao peoples, from the southwest of the province of Guizhou, in southeastern China, and also by the Han in the north.

Its composition is intriguing because of the ingenuity of the folds, which enable including compartments of different sizes superimposed in several layers. The paper used is washi, made with *Broussonettia papyrifera* fibers, a mulberry paper with good folding resistance.

"For more than a century, Chinese peasant women have saved threads and needles in folded paper envelopes. In several provinces, a new paper structure emerged, with unfoldable compartments that conceal and reveal more envelopes. This object is called *'zhen xian bao'*, which means 'needle over thread' and also 'play of threads' or 'book of hidden boxes'.

These structures might contain only a few compartments or more than a hundred. They are used to store sewing utensils such as thread, needles, dyed silk cocoons, horse mane, fabric samples and different embroidery patterns.

Over the course of a lifetime, it is common to keep pieces of daily objects in the compartments: family photographs, receipts, horoscopes, train tickets, change and family documents. Over time, a kind of private diary emerges.

Zhen xian bao are handmade, strikingly adorned, unique pieces created specially by each owner.

Many women consider them their most precious possession."
Ed Hutchins, August 2020.

• *Traditional style with mixed compartments..
This model is probably from Shanxi, a province in northern China. It is not common to combine different structures, but this piece includes twist and flower pockets. The first ones are decorated with rolls with peach jam, grapes, butterflies and crickets; the second ones are adorned with multicolor cut-paper flowers
On the surface are sixteen foldable pockets.
Each combination of two compartments opens to eight more pockets, each group of four to another four, each group of eight to two others and, finally, the two sides open to another pocket; in all, thirty-one different compartments.
Ed Hutchins
Format: folded, 28 x 16 cm (11 x 6 in); unfolded, 32 cm (13 in). Collection Book Architecture Resource Center, United States*

• *Dong-style dragon book*
"Popular among the Dong minority of Guizhou province, in southern China, dragon and fish illustrations are covered with Tung oil to make them harder. This model opens in two stages. First are eight spinning twist enclosures; then another eleven vertical compartments that fold."
Ed Hutchins
Format: folded, 27 x 15 cm (11 x 6 in); unfolded: 60 cm (24 in). Collection Book Architecture Resource Center, United States.

Contemporary variations

An essential book, *A Little Known Chinese Folk Art: Zhen Xian Bao* (Occidor Ltd, 2012), by Ruth Smith and Gina Corrigan, was crucial in the spread of this popular art that interests a wide range of contemporary artists. One of them is Paula Versnick, an origami enthusiast who on her website Orihouse, provides diagrams based on the studies of Joan Sallas, an expert folder, researcher and historian of folding, and Paula Beardell Krieg, who has published her research and other astonishing creations on her well-documented blog Bookzompa. The structure of the *"shu bao"* is very inspiring. It allows for variations in the assembly of horizontal and vertical compartments, as well as replacing the traditional chrysanthemum pattern with others such as the *tatô*, graceful Japanese pouches with geometric patterns.

📧 bookzoompa.wordpress.com/2016/10/22/inside-a-chinese-thread-book-zhen-xian-bao-post-7

📧 www.orihouse.com/zhenxianbao.html

📧 www.foldingdidactics.com/wp-content/uploads/2015/12/zhen_xian_beyo.pdf

📧 origamitutorials.com/origami-chinese-thread-book

• Kit contemporain, *Paula Beardell Krieg, 2017. Format: folded, 15.5 x 9 cm (6 x 4 in); unfolded, 38 cm (15 in).* "Includes several small overlapping envelopes, hidden folded compartments, a secret pocket and pages of text for recording notes and thoughts." *Ed Hutchins. Collection Book Architecture Resource Center, United States.*

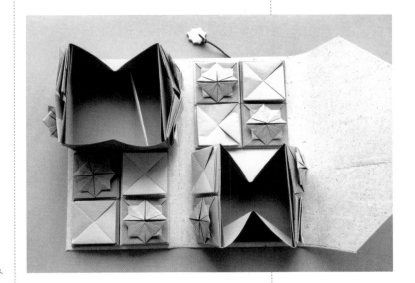

• Shu bao, J.-Ch. Trebbi, 2019.
Format: folded, 19 x 32 x 3.5 cm (7 x 13 x 1);
unfolded, 57 x 32 cm (22 x 13 in). Unique copy,
thirty compartments. This model, made of beige
Kraft paper, embodies two traditional patterns: the
chrysanthemum and Moroccan currency twist folds.

A card holder or wallet fold can serve as an easy base for making a book. The concept is simple: the pages are obtained from a strip of paper folded accordion style. Another folded strip is then added that functions as a cover.

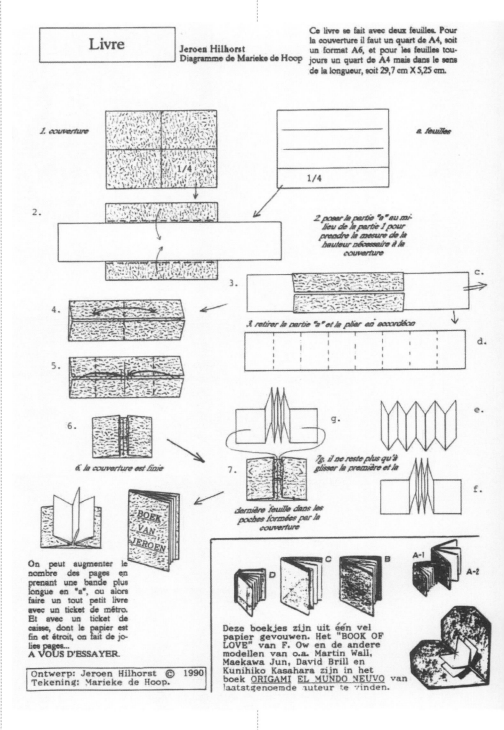

Ce livre se fait avec deux feuilles. Pour la couverture il faut un quart de A4, soit un format A6, et pour les feuilles toujours un quart de A4 mais dans le sens de la longueur, soit 29,7 cm X 5,25 cm.

Livre

Jeroen Hilhorst
Diagramme de Marieke de Hoop

1. couverture

a. feuilles

1/4

1/4

2. poser la partie "a" au milieu de la partie 1 pour prendre la mesure de la hauteur nécessaire à la couverture

3. retirer la partie "a" et la plier en accordéon

6. la couverture est finie

7g. il ne reste plus qu'à glisser la première et la dernière feuille dans les poches formées par la couverture

On peut augmenter le nombre des pages en prenant une bande plus longue en "a", ou alors faire un tout petit livre avec un ticket de métro. Et avec un ticket de caisse, dont le papier est fin et étroit, on fait de jolies pages...
A VOUS D'ESSAYER.

Ontwerp: Jeroen Hilhorst © 1990
Tekening: Marieke de Hoop.

Deze boekjes zijn uit één vel papier gevouwen. Het "BOOK OF LOVE" van F. Ow en de andere modellen van o.a. Martin Wall, Maekawa Jun, David Brill en Kunihiko Kasahara zijn in het boek ORIGAMI EL MUNDO NUEVO van laatstgenoemde auteur te vinden.

La revue du Mouvement Français
LE PLI
des Plieurs de Papier

Nº 47

ISSN 0240-0588

BONNES VACANCES 1991

• *Revista* Le Pli *no. 47, 1991, where the fold by Jeroen Hilhorst is shown with diagrams by Marieke de Hoop.*

Jeroen Hilhorst

BASQUE COUNTRY

"This book is made with two sheets. For the cover, paper one quarter the size of A4 (U.S. letter), in other words, A6 (4 $^{1/8}$ × 5 $^{7/8}$ in), is needed. The pages also require A4 (U.S. letter) format but lengthwise, or 29.7 × 5.25 cm (12 × 2 in). The number of pages can be increased using a longer strip."

A variation of this model is based on the reverse concept. In this case, the accordion-fold strip for the pages has an upper and lower fold, and the pages at the ends are inserted in a small cover strip. It is a good idea to anticipate a backlash of about 5 mm (2 in) at the center, depending on the thickness of the pages.

✏ mfpp-origami.fr/le-pli

✏ *Libri in un minuto*, Quaderni di quadrato magico no. 55, C.D.O. 2015. In this highly didactic document, Luosa Canovi presents some beautiful models, noteworthy for the simplicity of the folds.

✏ www.origami-do.it/luisa-canovi

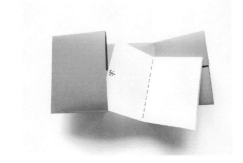

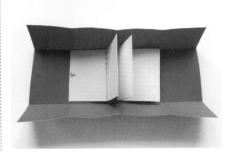

• *This easy-to-make model consists of a folded cover in which an accordion strip is inserted for the pages.*
(Creation of Jeroen Hilhorst, 1990)

■ LITTLE CARD WALLET BOOK

• This very simple model with a clever fold has won over the hearts of many folders and enthusiasts across the world, who probably do not know its creator's name. According to the type of paper and format chosen, surprising and amusing variations are possible. As a base for the books, many other card wallet or billfold models can be used. Among them, those by Martin Wall, Nick Robinson and Sok Song are easy to adapt. The smallest one is made with a 7.5 x 7.5 (3 x 3 in) square; final format 3 x 2 cm (4 x 0.8 in). (Created by J.-Ch. Trebbi, 2020.)

Humiako Huzita

JAPAN

A physicist born in Japan who decided to settle in Padua (Italy), Humiako Huzita (1924-2005) was an experienced origamist known for his *huzita-hatori* axioms and studies concerning the mathematics of paper folding.
This model was shown for the first time in 1988, at the CDO (Centro Diffusione Origami) convention, which brings together Italian origamists and enthusiasts.

📖 www.origami-cdo.it

📖 britishorigami.info/academic/lister/humiaki_huzita.php

   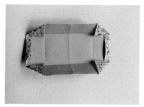

• The initial sheet of this billfold fold transformed into a little book/billfold is an A4 or A3 rectangle. The accordion-fold strip that forms the pages is inserted in the inside of the covers.
If the initial format is a 20 cm (8 in) square side, the result is a 5 x 9.5 cm (2 x 4 in) book.

If an A3 format is used (29.7 x 42 cm) (12 x 16.5 in), the final format will be 10.5 x 14 cm (4 x 5.5 in).
To facilitate the insertion, it helps if the fold is not made exactly parallel to the edge of the sheet. Starting with the same construction of folds, yet slightly modifying certain angles, the position of the billfold folds and the fitting together of the components, different patterns are obtained. Here we see variations obtained depending on the measurements of the initial sheet, whether it is two-tone or not (see opposing page).

■ ORIGAMI COVER AND INSERTION OF PAGES

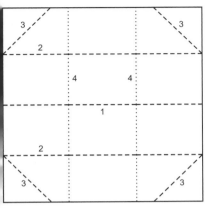

• Folded cover forming three two-tone parallel strips. The strip for the pages, folded accordion style, has two insertion slots on the cover. The strip that will serve as the cover is folded 1 cm (0.4 in) above and below lengthwise. At the end, it is folded 1 cm (0.4 in) vertically on the back. The strip is folded in two, and again in two.
Check for good insertion in the folds at the other end. Prepare the strip that you are going to fold in two according to the length of the book. Make two height cuts just above the upper and lower folds. Unfold the cover completely and insert the accordion strip, and then close it. Starting with an A4 format (10.5 x 29.7 cm) (4 x 12 in), a 7 x 7 cm (3 x 3 in) book is obtained. (Creation of J.-Ch. Trebbi)

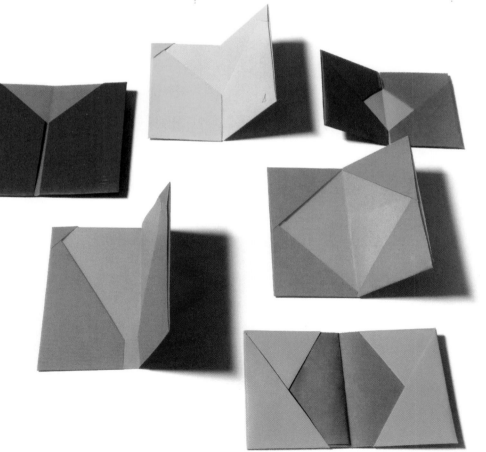

• A variation of the little card wallet book with a square base.. The accordion-fold strip of the pages is inserted in the back of the cover, which allows for different triangular patterns. Starting with a 20 x 20 cm (8 x 8 in) format, a 5 x 7 cm (2 x 3 in) mini book is obtained. (Creation of J.-Ch. Trebbi)

• *Inspired by the creations of Shuzo Fujimoto, this original variation of a sculpture book is made from distinctive V-shaped or herringbone folds. When it is folded, it has a triangular format; it can be also be exhibited unfolded, whether as a leporello or corolla book. It is folded with a single sheet of paper that can be complemented by a simple accordion fold on the back part. (Creation of J.-Ch. Trebbi, 2018).*

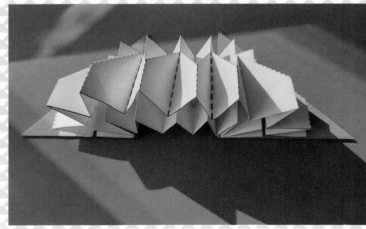

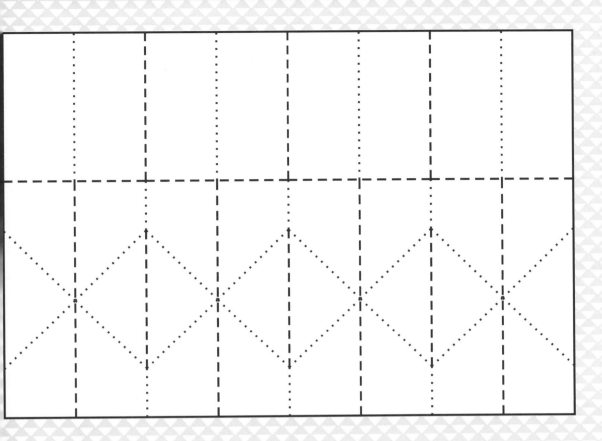

LITTLE BILLFOLD BOOK
MODEL 1-2-3

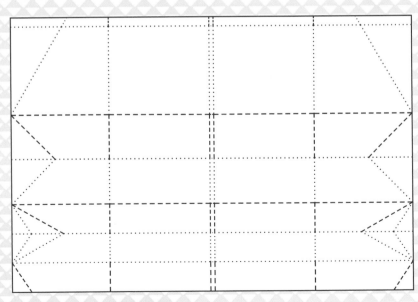

• Little billfold book with six side pockets and accordion-fold pages. (Creation of J.-Ch. Trebbi, 2019).

*"I assimilate what I see. I experiment,
I change course, I rebuild, I alternate.
I feel free to come up with structures
that have content beyond words and
images. I'm interested in giving life to
the book as a mechanical object of
extraordinary diversity."*
Hedi Kyle

kirigami

• Paravent des contes, *Frédérique Le Lous
Delpech, cover jacket by Julie Auzillon, 2015.*

PERIPHERAL CUTS

The term kirigami *is from the Japanese* kiru, *which means "to cut", and* kami, *"paper". Kiragimi, then, is the art of paper cutting. This chapter takes a look at books that contain all types of cuts: accordion books or cut-out leporellos, cut-out strips with inserted sheets, flag books with added pages, little books and paper cutouts that project and fractal books with diminishing pages.*

We will also find geographic and road maps with specific kinds of folds and cuts that serve as unexpected sources of inspiration.

■ LEPORELLO STRIP DIMINISHING CUT

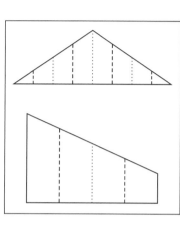

• Accordion strip with simple or symmetrical fold. The bias cut produces continuous map folds in relief.

• Into my Bodice, Annwyn Dean, 2015.
Three approximately 10 x 50 cm (4 x 20 in)
copies inspired by 19th century travel narratives.

• Chronotopic, Cartographies for Literature,
Kevin Steele, 2017-2018.
Format: folded, 25 x 22.5 x 0.6 cm; (10 x 9 x 0.2 in)
unfolded; 25 x 22.5 x 69 cm. (10 x 9 x 27 in)
*"When creating a concertina with various levels,
the structure allows us to reveal six types of literary
landscapes depending on the degree of reality or
fiction of each one, showing the theoretical links that
join them."*

• Val di Funes / Villnöss, *Kevin Steele, 2011.*
*Format: folded, 16.25 x 22.5 x 0.95 cm (6 x 9
x 4 in) unfolded: 122 x 22.5 x 16.25 cm (9 x
12 x 3 in).*
*"This silkscreen print accordion book depicts
a detachable alpine landscape that represents
a specific valley in northern Italy, strongly
influenced by German culture. The structure
is inspired by the great 19th century paper
engineer Lothar Meggendorfer and his book The
City Park. The work is intended to be immersive
and interactive; it invites the reader to fold the
pages in different directions to create their own
Southern Tyrol landscape."*

Laurence Bucourt

FRANCE

Laurence Bucourt is a calligraphy and plastic artist who participates regularly in different artist book fairs. She is the founder of the association Lettres & Images in Gradignan, Gironda (France), where she takes part in workshops.

"I often choose the accordion book technique because it lends itself to many variations when adding pages to the folds or joining them like in a flag book. Also, the other side can be used to make a two-sided book.

With a cut and a reversal of the folds, the book comes alive as a pop-up.

It also has the advantage of being able to be unfolded to provide a panoramic view, which transforms the book into an interesting object from the point of view of plasticity.

I choose the paper depending on the technique that I'm going to use, keeping in mind visual results that involve transparency, texture and color. My most common choice is 130 g/m² (48 lb) Ingres Arches MBM® laid paper sheets.

Soft to the touch and sight, white without being frigid, it lends itself well to embossing and cutting, and its light texture is good for my pen marks. I also like 110 g/m² (41 lb) elephant-skin paper for its resistance, flexibility and dappled tones. It's very smooth and adapts well to the folds. The dust jackets and covers of my books can be made from strong paper, photographic paper or binding cardboard. The sleeves for storing and protecting my books are made from 300 g/m² (111 lb) black photographic paper.

• Plus loin, 2013.
Format: folded, 15.5 x 20 x 0.8 cm (6 x 8 x 0.3 in); unfolded, 40 x 25 x 20 cm (16 x 10 x 8 in). Accordion book with cutting. Text of medieval songs of Santiago de Compostela pilgrims, in Latin. 130 g/m² (48 lb) Ingres Arches MBM paper. The simple hinged cover is made of wood pulp board covered with Nepal paper.

For the book we see above, my intention was to follow the text closely, to transcribe the idea of an ascending road and its spiritual dimension through the vertical quality of the format, ensuring that the text and image could be seen in their entirety. Cutting and calligraphy are two aesthetically close techniques, and I wanted to have them enter into a dialogue with each other.

This accordion book is made up of five 15 cm (6 in) sections each, cut with a cutter in the upper part following the form of the calligraphy letters or the outlines of the landscapes bordering the road. The height of each page is slightly greater than the one before it. As a result, when the book is half opened or flat, the ascending road is shown. Some supplementary cuts are added in the lower part of the unwritten pages.

The highest page, which is the last page of the book, is joined to the cover on the flap of the binding. This makes the white outlines stand out against the dark blue background of the cover."
Laurence Bucourt, December 2019.

📖 laurencebucourt.com

■ STRIP WITH TRIANGULAR FOLD

GINA PISELLO

"One day, while I was in a restaurant waiting for my order, I entertained myself with the paper wrapping drinking straws come in. I often distract myself with pieces of fallen paper. I fold them to see what happens when I handle them. The fineness and length of the paper around the straws allowed me to fold it and roll it around itself. And that's how I came up with the prototype of this book. I like that it only has two pages, that its center allows it to remain standing, and that the two sides of the paper are visible once the folding is completed.

As for the printing technique, I used color spray ink to dye the white paper before folding it. I chose two slightly different inks for the two sides to create contrast, and I wrote two versions in haiku. I like to use handcrafted materials and pens to create the color and content of my books. They are accessible easy-to-use materials."
Gina Pisello.

• Straw fold book, *Gina Pisello, 2015. Made with a 5.8 x 58.5 cm (2 x 23 in) strip, folded format on a square with 5.6 cm (2 in) sides.*

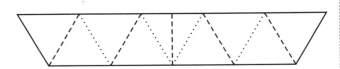

• *A simple strip made up of equilateral triangles folded over themselves in alternating fashion results in a final model with a square base. Structure and diagram, Gina Pisello, 2015.*

■ STRIP WITH CIRCULAR BASE

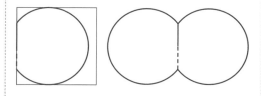

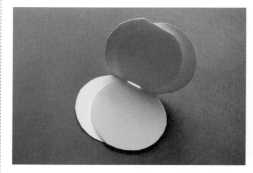

• *After folding the sheet in two, the pages are cut in a circular shape according to the desired model. Then all you need to do is make a slit halfway up in the central fold to fit the little sheets together.*

■ VARIATION WITH IRREGULAR BASE

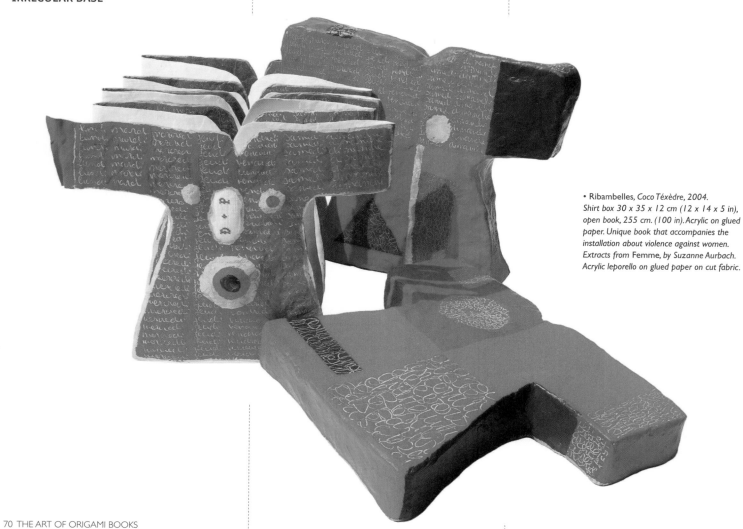

• *Ribambelles,* Coco Téxèdre, *2004.*
Shirt box 30 x 35 x 12 cm (12 x 14 x 5 in), open book, 255 cm. (100 in). Acrylic on glued paper. Unique book that accompanies the installation about violence against women. Extracts from Femme, *by Suzanne Aurbach. Acrylic leporello on glued paper on cut fabric.*

Miyako Akai

JAPAN

Miyako Akai began writing while studying architecture. Since 2001, he has been making books for his texts. As his stories have grown shorter, the formats of the books have decreased, becoming authentic architectural miniatures.

His interest in working with covers has captured the attention of numerous Japanese media organizations. He has been a member of the Miniature Book Society since 2007.

"Offering a miniature book is something more intimate than presenting a normal size one. It's like whispering instead of speaking." *Miyako Akai, December 2019.*

✆ kototsubo.com

• Canned circular book, 2011.
"*I decided to put the book in a can. When the can is opened, the spirals emerge in a beautiful and savage way, but the book can break if it's twisted too much. I chose old violin music paper and decorated it with pressed flowers. I glued some pieces of paper in the folds to strengthen them. This structure is very uncommon, but it works extremely well.*"

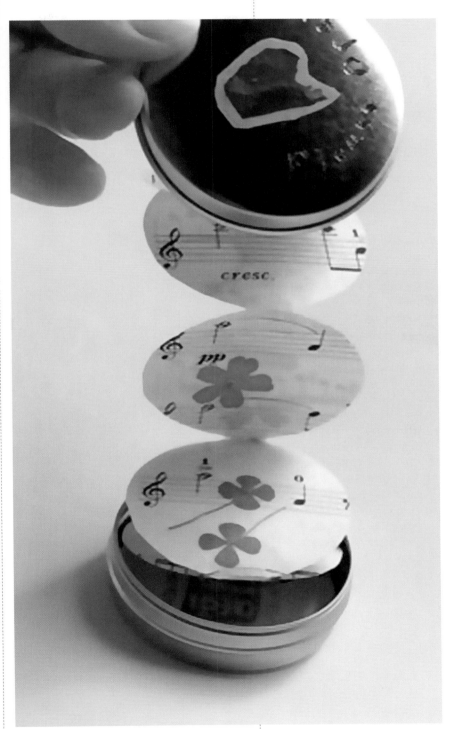

Emile Goozairow

RUSSIA

Born in 1961, Emile Goozairow is an author, poet, designer, illustrator and graphic artist. He produces animated movies, trailers and music clips. Emile is a multifaceted artist, and the miniature book is one of his passions. In it, he skillfully uses different materials not usually associated with this form. He is convinced that each book has its own scale: some have to be big and others small. As a result, his creations are of different sizes, from very large to very small.

"I almost always start by drawing a series of illustrations related to the subject matter of my future book. I reflect while I design. Then I write the text that will go with the drawings. It's the best strategy for me. I call it *reverse illustration*'. Usually, illustrators illustrate preexisting texts. I do the contrary, unless it's a book by classical authors such as T.S. Eliot, Edgar Allan Poe, Alexandre Pushkin or William Shakespeare...

I make an effort not to take anything from other artists and to do everything myself. I work with Photoshop for my drawings. I do the layout and choose the font. Later, I print the pages in high definition, unless I use a professional printer.

For the binding, I tend to use fabrics, polymer pulp, handmade felt and silver elements. Then I fit it all together. I can spend a lot of time creating models and conducting tests."

Emile Goozairow, January 2020.

🖎 www.goozairow.com

🖎 www.behance.net/emilguzair4cc4

• Agathon's Apparatus, *2020.*
"A series of small stories about the way in which Agafon Boke finds different objects at the seashore, including a dream projector, a thought recorder and many more. At the end of the story, he encounters a large fair of unknown devices."

- Emile Goozairow in his workshop.
- Start of cutting and folding on a hexagonal base.

• The Secret Lexicon, 2018.

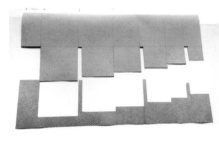

• Concertina coloré, J.-Ch.Trebbi, 2019.
14 cm (5.5 in) diagonal, hexagon format in
brown Kraft box This playful kinetic structure
is made up of eight pages that unfold in
chrromatic order. Installed at a height of 50 cm
(20 in) on a work plan, the concertina unfolds in
a vibrant cascade of colors.

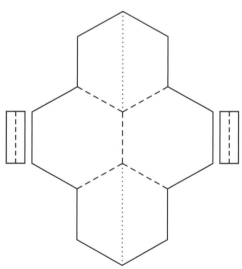

• Fractal book. The creases, folds and peripheral
cuts form a little book with pockets and
diminishing pages.
"I wanted to make a book without binding,
always from a single sheet of a paper but with
increasing pages. I called it a 'fractal book'.
The method is simple: it consists of folding the
paper in two, reproducing the drawing of the
cutout, cutting the combined elements and
marking the folds according to the instructions."
(Creation of J.-Ch.Trebbi, 2019).

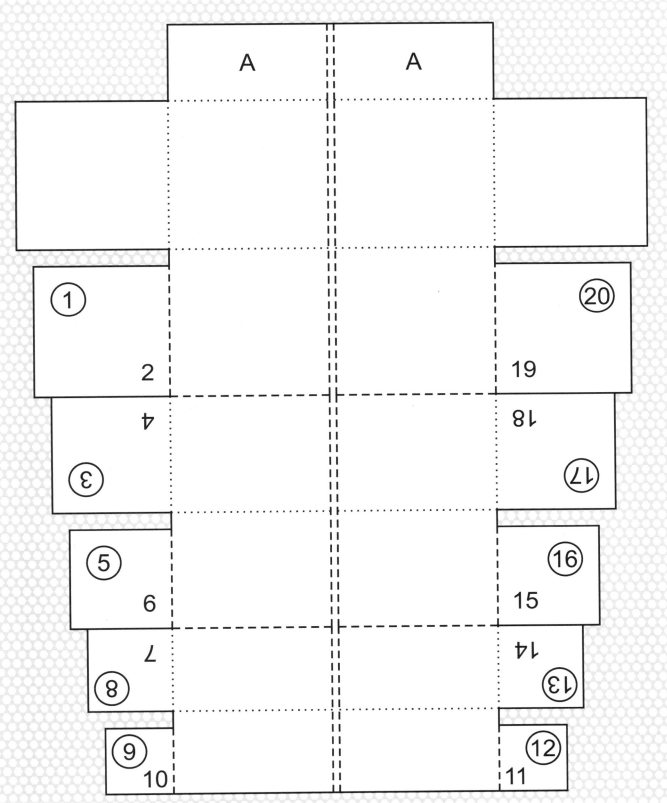

CENTRAL CUTS INCISIONS OR SLOTS

"When I come up with the idea for a book, I often go about it in the same way: 1: choice of the base idea, the subject matter I want to focus on and for which I make a preliminary sketch. 2: defining and choice of the production technique. 3: creation of printer's dummy, to check compatibility with the image and choice of paper I'm looking for. 4: more or less numerous adaptations, finalizing, cutting, addition of elements. 5: final production by manual cut (with scalpels or cutters with different blades) incorporating the trials and errors in a single piece that is the definitive prototype. 6: possible use of numerical or laser cut according to the delicacy of the cut or the number of copies (less than ten).

My tools are basic: crayons, felts, rulers, stilettos, old pens, adhesives, cutters, scapels, compass, draftsman's square, tweezers, circular cutter, hole puncher, bamboo rod... I use them with pleasure, according to how I want to use them. In contrast, when it comes to the paper, I have very clear preferences. I like Hahnemühl bamboo paper and Nostalgie paper, because of its fine grain and broken white color. I also like Sugar Cane de Lana for its granular texture and sometimes handicraft papers by French paper manufacturers, Kraft, carbon copy, gray, white and colored cardboard... I have a large inventory because I compulsively purchase papers I like, even though at the time I'm not sure what I'm going to use them for!

What's great about this material is that anything is possible, everything can be done. There aren't any limits in size, color, assembly or binding.

I rarely make the same thing twice, because I'm interested more than anything in the search for different creative possibilities. But technique and creation are closely linked. In the adaptation of the model, and often in the improvements made to it, there are endless comings and goings. It gives me immense pleasure to search for and find different forms of installation, as well as exploring the techniques invented by the pioneers of the genre.

Often I establish a product specification for the project. Certainly, it's a *déformation professionnelle* from my previous life as an architect, who must be sensitive to the client's demands. Still, it helps me to establish a framework and also is a kind of challenge, although sometimes the impositions are adapted to the type of paper or to my mood at the time."

✆ www.orilum.com

• Angel dance, 2011. Double leporello made of colored paper cutouts.
Format: 31 x 32 cm (4 x 0.8 in).
The fitting method we see here creates a kind of hinge that provides much more flexibility than a piece of adhesive tape.

■ DOUBLE OR TRIPLE CONCERTINA

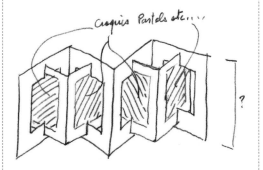

Croquis Pastels etc....

• The double concertina is obtained by fitting together two accordion-fold strips in which a slit has been made halfway up. The strip that contains the background has the slits going up and the other strip has them going down. This technique is similar to that of slice forms applied to pop-up books. This system offers a great deal of flexibility when folding the structure up small, since each assembly functions as a hinge.
Attention needs to be paid to the slits, whose width must be suitable for the thickness of the paper used.

• Double concertina center pages fit together, model by J.-Ch. Trebbi, creation of J.-C. Planchenault.
The bearing strip that serves as a background has several rectangular cuts that extend up and down with vertical slits in the center of the rectangles, allowing for the overlay of the front strip.

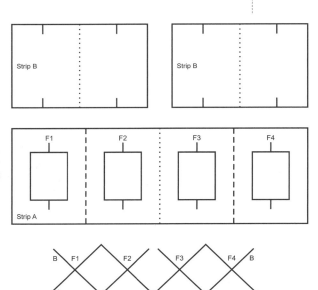

4 x 4 GRID FOLD AND V CUT

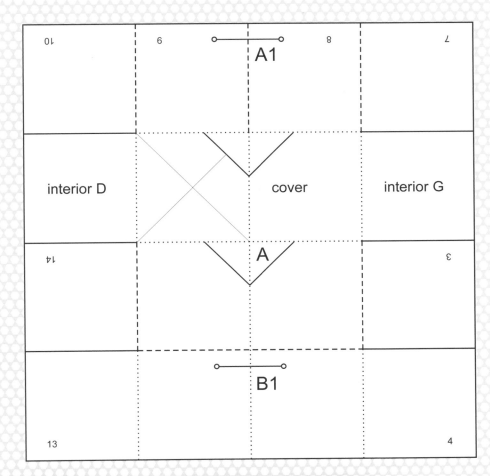

interior D   cover   interior G

A1

A

B1

• *Starting from a square base, the small central triangular cuts on a 4 x 4 grid guarantee blocking of the pages. Fold a 4 x 4 grid. Then mark the cut lines like in the drawing.*
Trick: to avoid tears, puncture the angles of the cuts with a very small hole puncher.
Fold the sheet in two, folding the 13-4 part over the 10-7. Insert tab B into B1. Fold the upper strip downward. Insert tab A into A1. Join the sides and fold over the central axis.
With a 20 x 20 cm (8 x 8 in) sheet of a paper, a 5 x 5 cm (2 x 2 in) mini book is obtained. (Creation of J.-Ch. Trebbi, 2019.)

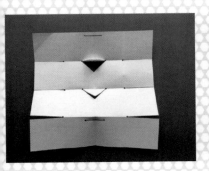

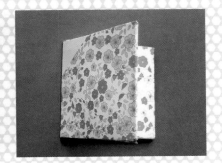

■ V CUTS, "GOOSE FOOT"
FOUR FEET, 16 PAGES

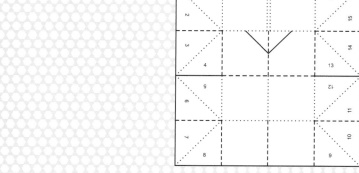

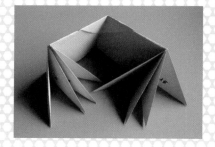

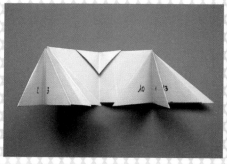

■ V CUTS "GOOSE FOOT"
THREE FEET, 14 PAGES

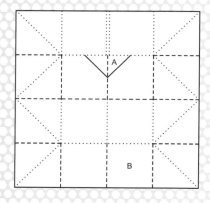

• Using the same square base, folded from a 4 x 4 grid, then folded accordion style according to the diagram and folding of the ends to form triangles. The central V slit is a variation. (Creation of J.-Ch. Trebbi, 2019).

• This model is a variation of the previous one. The central slit forms a blocking mechanism and the two side cuts allow for a book with sixteen pages.

LOHNES BOOK, ACCORDION BASE

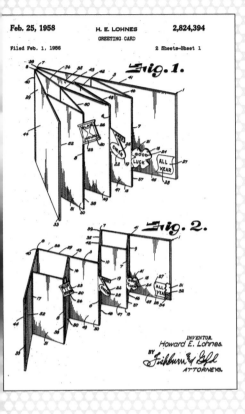

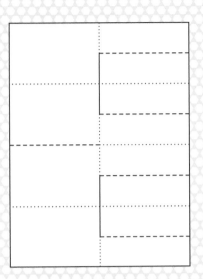

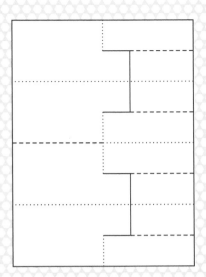

• This interesting model is inspired by the greeting card created in 1956 by Howard E. Lohnes, of Kansas City, for the company Hallmark. It has two central slits and tab instructions to make the accordion-fold pages with illustrations project out.
Folded from a 4 x 2 grid and creation of a partial cuts to make an eight-page book.

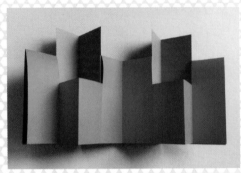

• The two central cuts are offset to the sides of the central axis, creating two projecting areas when folded.

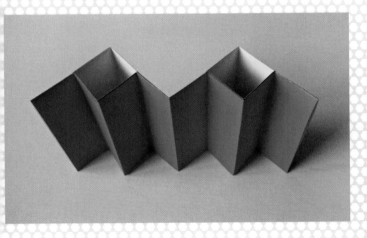

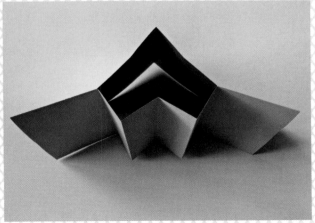

■ FRENCH DOORS

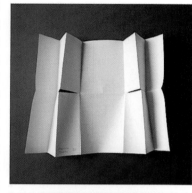

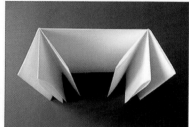

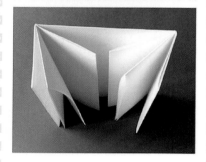

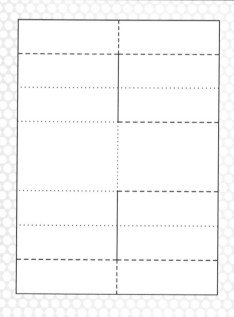

• Despite being made with a single folded sheet of paper, this beautiful structure created by Ed Hutchins gives the impression of consisting of two books side by side.

■ FLAG BOOK

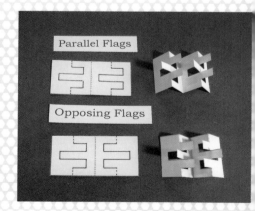

Parallel Flags

Opposing Flags

• The flag book model, created by the prolific artist Hedi Kyle, consists of the combination of an accordion-fold strip format. Pieces of page that form small flags are placed over the pages alternatively and from left to right. Model recreated by J-Ch. Trebbi from a single folded and cut sheet and a parallel flag proposed by Ed Hutchins.

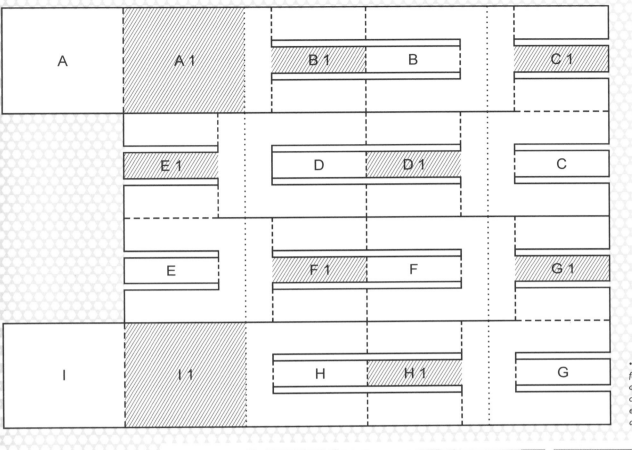

| A | A1 | B1 | B | C1 |

| E1 | D | D1 | C |

| E | F1 | F | G1 |

| I | I1 | H | H1 | G |

• Another flag book model, also from a single sheet of paper, designed by Ed Hutchins. This concept is intended for more experienced folders. Some parts are joined two by two.

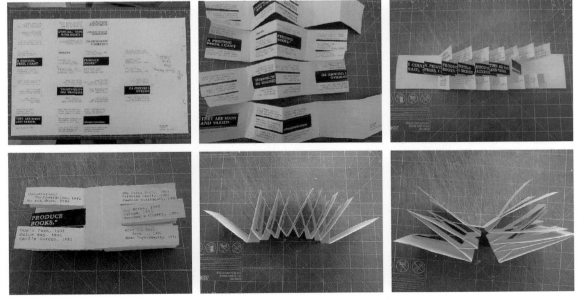

Gisela Oberbeck

GERMANY

Gisela lives and works in Munich. Subtly
and masterfully, the artist uses an extensive
palette of techniques: wood engraving,
stamping, painting and collage.
She participates regularly in artist book fairs
all over the world.

"For many years, I've been interested in
cutting as a means of artistic expression,
both in wood and paper.
In the series *"Recueillir les ombres"*, I
introduce shadows in the book to release
them through cutting.
Exploring landscapes of shadows, I draw
on blank leporellos. I collect impressions
of places. Later, I begin a long and delicate
process in the studio. There I decide what
I'm going to cut in the preliminary drawing,
what's going to appear in the composition
and how the pages are going to be
combined. This also allows me to tell the
stories of the places, developing a subtle
play of moving forms, shadows and light.
Gisela Oberbeck, May 2020.

✉ www.gisela-oberbeck-go.com

• Jardin d'Eden perturbé, 2009.
*Format: folded, 20 x 52 cm; (8 x 20.5 in);
unfolded: 220 x 52 cm (87 x 20.5 in).*
"After the angel expelled man from Paradise,
the angel saw he was depressed. Man had
disappeared as part of the whole."

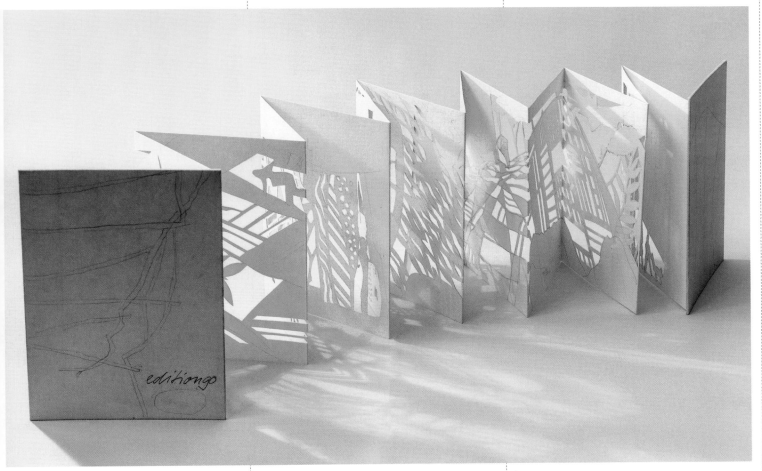

• NYC, 2010.
Format: folded, 20 x 52 cm (8 x 20.5 in);
unfolded, 220 x 52 cm (87 x 20.5 in).
"This work transforms real shadows and
impressions of New York visions into a series of
light and shadow with always changing reflections."

• Paisaje de d'ombre et sable, 2014.
Format: folded, 13 x 18 cm (5 x 7 in); unfolded:
180 x 18 cm (4 x 0.8 in).
"Print of a landscape in the United States
with the poem by Amy Lowell 'Shore of Lake
Michigan'."

Béatrice Coron

UNITED STATES

Born in France, Béatrice Coron has lived and worked in New York for thirty years. She needs no introduction. Much of her work forms part of numerous collections in prestigious places.

Her creations tell stories of everyday life, cities and fantasy worlds where she makes unlikely juxtapositions cut in Tyvek®, an unwoven material.

"My silhouettes are a language I've developed over the years. My point of view is detailed and monumental at the same time. Cut in a single piece of material, the profusion of stories creates a coherent universe.
In my artist books and public art, where I play with full and empty forms, everything must be situated in its proper place, its place in the city, its place on the body.
In my graphic style, windows are used not to see the exterior but the interior, placing the viewer in an *outsider/insider* situation. The shadows, which recall film noir and voyeurism, leave space for multiple interpretations."
Béatrice Coron, December 2019.

✎ www.beatricecoron.com/french.html

• Daphnis & Chloé: Eternal return, *2014, cut Tyvek, 140 x 14 cm (55 x 5.5 in).*

• Machines, *2017. Poem by Michael Donaghy. Format: 19 x 11 cm (4 x 0.8 in). Paper Arches.*

• Memory Holes, *2014. Format: 74 x 19 cm (4 x 0.8 in). Paper Arches.*

• The Artist books' path, *2016. Format: 19 x 112 cm (4 x 0.8 in). Paper Arches.*

■ SIDE CUT AND AT AN ANGLE : *CORNER CUT* AND *SIDE CUT*

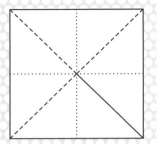
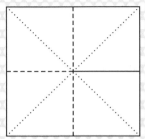

• How do you make triangular books? Here are three variations made by starting with a square base, proposed by Ed Hutchins. The difference is in the placement of the partial cut, which can be a side cut or crossed at one of the angles.

■ ED TRIANGLE BASE: RIZA SANTOS MODEL

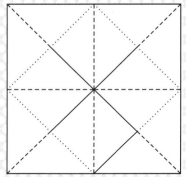

FOLDED BOOKLET

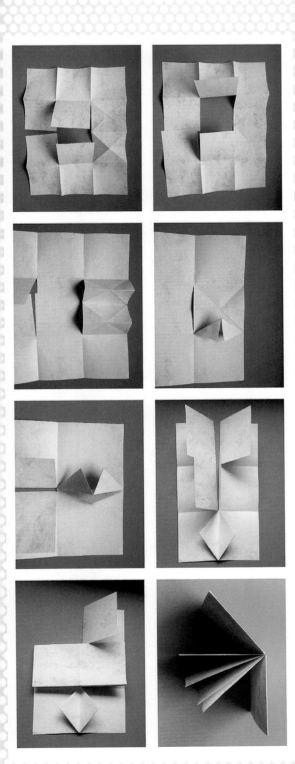

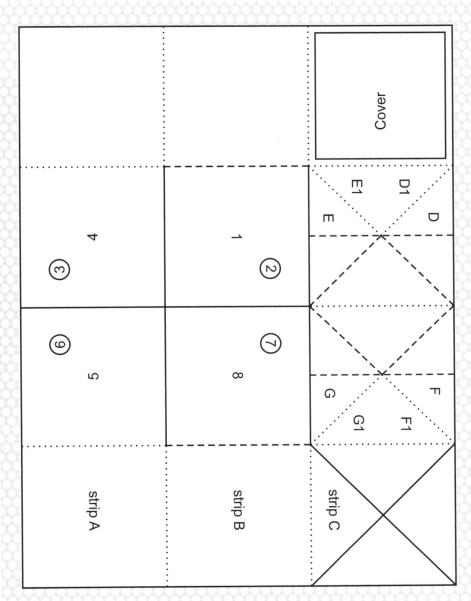

• Eight-page booklet with a central fold.
It is recommended to number the pages in pencil to be able to see the order of the central block folds.
1- Mark the folds and make the cuts.
2- Fold strip A under strip B.
3- Fold sides 8-5 to the right and 1-4 to the left.
4- Turn the object over.
5- Form blocking triangles in the center by moving F over F1 and G over G1; then, symmetrically, D over D1 and E over E1.
6- The result is a central rhombus positioned over the axis of the booklet and surrounded by pages 4 and 5.
7- Fold the high part over the lower square.
8- Close the booklet by folding page 4 over page 5.
(Creation of J.-Ch. Trebbi).

"In my search for forms and the folding ability of book structures, I became interested in road map folds, which provide us with some hints about the subject. I chose the original model by Stacy E. Boyer (Casper, Wyoming), who registered the patent in 1922. This model is based on a 6 × 8 grid and has folded longitudinal and transversal lines that divide the sheet in a variety of quadrants for the preparation of forty-eight pages. Several slots placed on the folded sheet in a zig-zag pattern enable the folded sections to be turned. This folding system is more complex than that of Gerhard Ernst Albrecht Falk. From Hamburg, in 1948 Falk invented a practical and intelligent system that does not require unfolding the entire map but rather provides a view by zones. The continuity of vision of the map is achieved by turning the previously folded and cut pages in all directions.
This model, called Falkplan, is used worldwide today."
J.-Ch. Trebbi

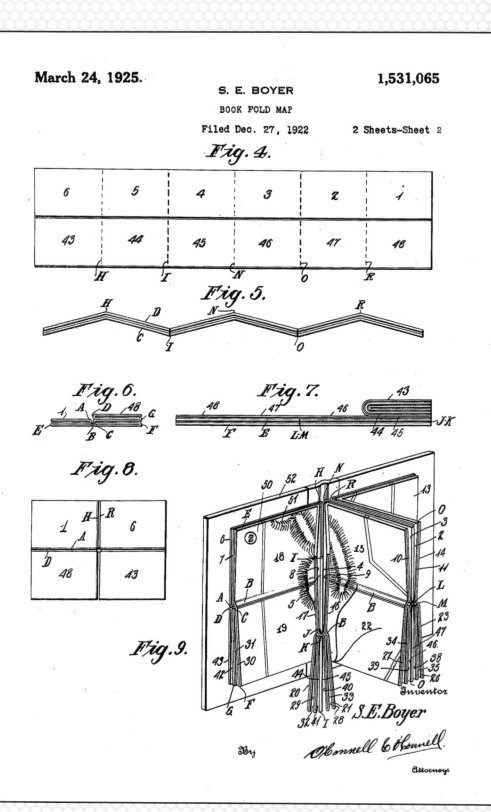

	H	I	N	O	R	
1	6	5	4	3	2	1
A						A
	7	8	9 (J)	10	11 (L)	12
E						E
2	18	17	16	15	14	13
B						B
	19	20	21	22	23	24
F						F
3	30	29	28	27	26	25
C						C
	31	32	33	34	35	36
G						G
4	42	41	40	39	38	37
D		(K)		(M)		D
	43	44	45	46	47	48
	H	I	N	O	R	

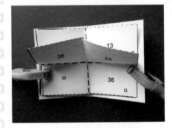

• This model, somewhat complicated to prepare, can be read from right to left and vice versa, thanks to the rise and fall of the pages. It's a fun challenge for experienced folders!
Fold in valley folds: AA, BB, CC, DD.
Fold in mountain folds: EE, FF, GG.
Cut along JK and LM lines.
Open by fold 2; fold between 18-17 in a valley fold and between 17-16 in a mountain fold.

Unfold the map and then pre-glue the entire back except for pages 6, 1, 43 and 48, which are the four rectangles at the ends that will be glued to the cover.
To read the map, it is best to go down the pages and then up the sides according to the numbering.
Once you get to page 12, lift the side, turn the page to the left, go up again and repeat.

FITTING THE PAGES TOGETHER

■ **FOLDED STRIP**
 SIMPLE FIT TOGETHER PAGES
 CENTRAL SLOT
 PRESTO MODEL

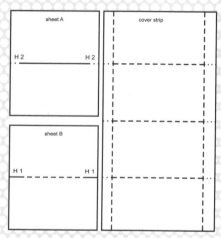

"A few years ago, my friend Claudine Pissale, origami sensei, former teacher, lover of the plastic arts and multi-talented person who loves to share her artistic discoveries, showed me this model by an unknown author. The fold interested me immediately for its intelligent and efficient fitting system.

It consists of a sheet that serves as a support, folded in two and with a partial cut in the middle, on the middle line.

The sheets also have cuts but in the upper and lower part. They are rolled halfway and inserted in the central slit of the support sheet.

The sheets at the ends are inserted later in a strip that functions as the cover, with folds above and below. I've also made other versions adding a supplementary fold in the cover and creating a small central rib for the Rapido model and large rib for the Nervura."

J.-Ch. Trebbi

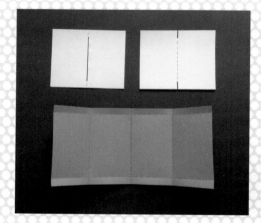

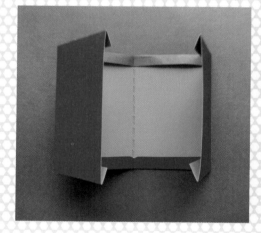

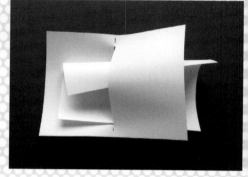

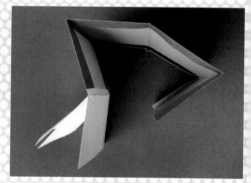

■ FIT TOGETHER PAGES
SMALL CENTRAL RIB
RAPIDO

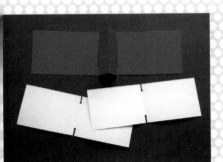

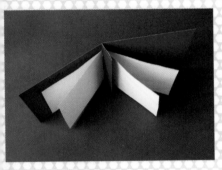

• The idea behind it is to simplify the Presto model. For this, it suffices to create an additional central rib that will function as a support for the pages. The width of the central slot must allow for covering the thickness of the pages to be inserted.
(Creation of J.-Ch. Trebbi, 2019).

■ SEPARATE SHEETS
FIT TOGETHER
PRESTO BACK TO BACK

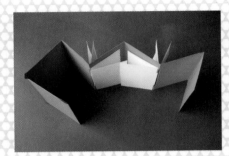

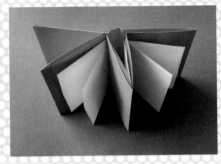

• The accordion-fold cover strip has two parallel slots. The pages fit together like in the Presto.

■ FIT TOGETHER SHEETS
INDEPENDENT
LARGE CENTRAL RIB
RAPIDO XL

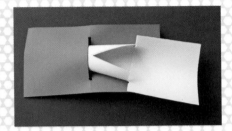

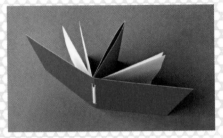

• The cover strip is folded toward the interior of the book forming a large central rib. This has a slot parallel to the central fold and serves as a support for the sheets that are inserted later. Pages can also be added by making several parallel slots. (Rib)

■ LARGE RIB
TWO PARALLEL SLOTS
NERVURA

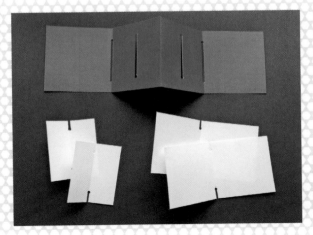

• A large central rib with two offset vertical slots that support the pages. This dynamic structure offers two page positions in such a way that the large ones envelop the small central pages.
(Creation of J.-Ch. Trebbi, 2019).

MIXED TECHNIQUES

■ **LEPORELLO AND PROJECTIONS**

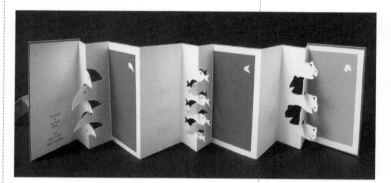

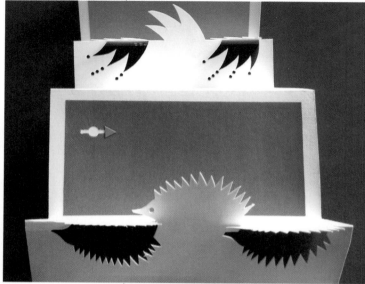

• *Regards, series of three booklets: Regards croisés, Regards marins, Regards piquants, J.-Ch. Trebbi, 2011.*
Folded format: 8.5 x 16 cm (4 x 0.8 in). Paper cutout and colored fabric leporello. Created by Édition l'Atelier du Milieu. Fabric binding by Marjon Mudde. It is closed by a small soft leather strip with a bead. Each cover is unique.

• Papivore, J.-Ch. Trebbi, 2011.
Cut leporello. Letters made by laser cut.
Format: 12.5 x 15 cm (4 x 0.8 in).
"Production of a leporello in which the letters
of the word 'papivore' (lit., papelí voro, 'paper
eater') are cut as if they had been devoured
by the insects that eat the books in my library.
Yet, according to the dictionary, the word also
refers to a 'person who reads or consumes a lot
of paper', and not, as a child asked his mother
when seeing my book at a fair: Is a 'papivoro' a
poppy (old man, grandpa) who eats children?"

■ LEPORELLO, FIT TOGETHER SHEETS AND PROJECTIONS

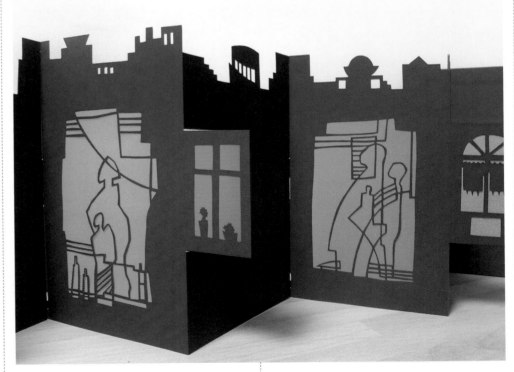

• Regards sur la ville, J.-Ch. Trebbi, 2013.
Format: folded, 30 x 31 cm (12 x 12 in); unfolded,
approx. 85 cm (33 in). Large book made of
black poster board, with two flags projecting out
from the page, showing the silhouettes of cities.
Progressive scene created by tinted windows that
light up when it gets dark. To be seen close to a
light source.

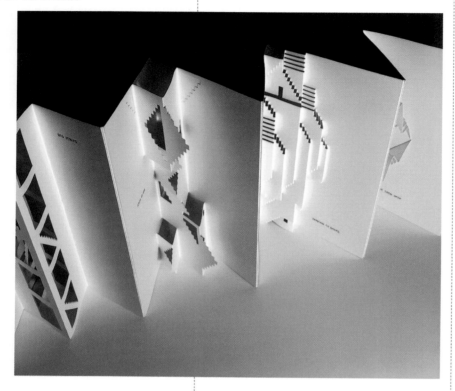

Nicolas Codron

FRANCE

Nicolas is an author, illustrator and paper engineer. This old rare book collector and merchant has a deep interest in art, music and languages and creates refined, highly graphic leporellos.

"This series of Steps, in addition to *footsteps* and *steps on stairs*, represents and manifests variations on the loss and rediscovery of oneself and the other, in mazes of imaginary stairs on the one hand and dreamed ones on the other: initiation games that one must go through. Each work is accompanied by a brief text, a prose poem, the first in French and the second in English.

These works are somewhere between the traditional book and the object book. They lend themselves well to sequential, diachronic, page by page reading or comprehensive synchronic reading in leporello format. The integral nature of the experience is visible at a glance. Time and reason are abolished, providing space, possibly, for the reader-spectator to wander." *Nicolas Codron, May 2020.*

🖙 nc-paperworks.blogspot.com

• Steps 2: More steps, 2017.
Format: folded, 20 x 15 x 3.5 cm (5 x 6.5 x1 in); unfolded: 20 x 120 cm (4 x 0.8 in). Artist book with system (kiri-origamic architecture), made totally by hand (cut Bristol paper, colored paper). Pop-up book with six double pages. It can be unfolded as a leporello (accordion book). Rigid cover with flaps, sleeve. 20 variations, numbered and signed.

J.-Ch.Trebbi

FRANCE

"I've always been very interested in graphology. For a long time, I had the idea of creating an alphabet. After defining the height, I prepared a representation protocol of the forms of the shafts (the vertical part), the crosspieces (horizontal parts) and the diagonal parts, which later I completed with the adaptation of the curved parts. The alphabet took form thanks to a series of trial and error, just like in the creation of all animated books and pop-up cards."

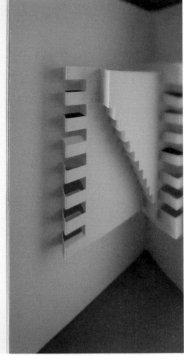

• AA, alphabet architectural, 2013. Leporello artist book. Computerized cut on Nostalgie Hahnemühle paper and Sugar Cane de Lana paper cover binding.
Format: folded, 15.5 x 17 x 5 cm (6 x 7 x 2 in); folded, 4.50 m (15 ft).

• Penseurs de villes, 2009.
Folded format: 17 x 24 cm (4 x 0.8 in). Leporello color paper cutouts on bamboo and sugar cane paper, ink drawings.

• Princes et princesses, 2009.
Format: folded, 17 x 24 cm (7 x 9 in); unfolded, 1.10 m (3.6 ft).
A medieval story without words conveyed by a leporello book and Hahnemühle Bamboo paper cutout pop-ups.

• Mini-Envol and Rébus, J.-Ch.Trebbi, 2013.
Unfolded format: 4.8 x 17 cm (2 x 7 in); box: 3.6 x 5.2 x 1.2 cm (9 x 12 x 3 in).

Brigitte Husson

FRANCE

"Brigitte Brendel Husson explored the world of the artist book with the curiosity of a child. Opening one of her books casts a spell, the beginning of a fairy tale journey. Her stories are filled with poetic characters, her scenery rendered like lace work with a cutter; the pages are folded, joined or juxtaposed to hide a word, a drawing, The imagery of her writing, the delicacy of the colors she uses, and the freedom of her dreams transport us to her dream world.

Accordion books, miniatures, box books, cut, suspended. She never put any limits on shape or size. She was daring with all materials, from precious papers to small everyday treasures accumulated over the years. With all freedoms granted, each one of her creations is a unique and original work of art."
Chantal Leibenguth, June 2020, Asociación Am'arts.

This association, which seeks to promote art and support artists, organizes exhibitions such as the Délires de Livres biennial, which presents object books and artist books (Chartres, Rambouillet, Viroflay).
In 2015, the exhibition Délires de Livres at Saint-André de Chartres college was dedicated to Brigitte Brendel Husson, who died in 2014.

✏ www.am-arts.com

• Enfin trouvés, 2019. Format: 10 x 60 cm (4 x 24 in), creation on two sides, Indian ink and watercolor on paper cutout.

• Attendre la première caresse du soleil et partir, 2012. Large leporello, approx. 15 x 120 cm (6 x 47 in), partial view, Indian ink and watercolor on paper cutout, two sides.

Isabelle Faivre

FRANCE

After training as a painter and decorator in Chantilly, Isabelle worked for fifteen years on television animation series and made her own short films such as *Du zéro des arènes*, nominated for the Berlin Golden Bear award in 1997. Isabelle has always chosen paper as a medium of expression, exchanging the pencil for the scalpel. With it, she carves and chisels astonishing white book sculptures, a unique creative process that challenges the elemental balances of volume. She moves comfortably from tiny to monumental works such as the submarine scenery she created for a showcase at the Viaduc des Arts in Paris.

She exhibits regularly in France. The small art magazine *Regard* dedicated its December 2016 issue to her.

"Trees, forests, plants and flowers are fashioned out of white paper and painted in shimmering colors. The lace-maker with the scalpel, the painter with the easel, the same artist brimming with inexhaustible creativity. Fabric, gouache, wood, photography and play are all part of her palette. Her artist books, whether enormous or minuscule, pristine or colored, bend in the face all restraints, which become inspirations. Nature is never far away; the city is adorned cinematically. It is said that she defies all expectations."
Text by Marie-Christine Guyonnet,
La Librairie du Ciel, May 2020.

🖝 meslivresinsolites.blogspot.fr

🖝 isabellefaivrepari.wixsite.com/artistepapier

• Théâtre du Zen, *2019. Mini diorama made from colored paper cutouts. Folded format: 4.5 x 6 cm (4 x 0.8 in).*

• Abécédaire, *2011. Miniature leporello printed and cut by hand. Format: folded, 6 x 5 x 1 cm (2 x 2 x 0.4 in); unfolded, approx. 70 cm (27.5 in).*

• J'annonce la couleur, *2011. Miniature leporello of proverbs related to color; gouache, cut, fold. Format: folded, 5.5 x 8.5 x 2 cm (2 x 2 x 0.4 in); unfolded, approx. 50 cm (27.5 in).*

• *Small leporello made in school workshops.*

Galerie MiniMa

FRANCE

Miniature, minuscule, microscopic, microbe, small-size books. A captivating and very special universe in which book artists must show great technical mastery and genuine skill. But what kind of books are hidden behind these names?

Catherine Okuyama, of MiniMa gallery, a specialist in small-format artist books, explains to us the characteristics of these uncommon creations:

"Miniature books are a very special and marginal part of publishing and have existed for thousands of years. In the Middle Ages, minuscule portable prayer books, psalteries, books of hours and even Bibles and Korans were published. Later, portable libraries easy to take on journeys were created. Thanks to their small size, these volumes could be hidden. For this reason, it was possible to preserve prohibited, religious, political and even erotic texts.

They are classified by size. Miniature books or small-size books can have a maximum measurement of 100 mm (4 in). In Japan, they can be up to 120 mm (5 in).

The measurements of tiny books or 64ths should not exceed 76 mm, according to the strict Anglo-Saxon standard (3 inches). There are even smaller ones called *microbes*, which are less than 15 mm (0.6 in) and can only be read with a magnifying glass."

"Miniature books are highly appreciated in

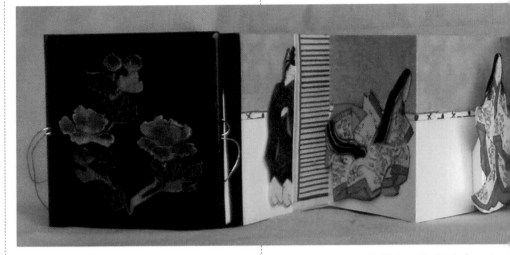

the world of origami. They are called *mame-hon* (pronounced *maméhon* or *mamébon*, literally 'bean book', a term that is generally translated as 'miniature book' and that corresponds to the tiny book or Western miniature (that is, 76 mm (3 in) as the maximum length of the longest side).

The word took on a uniquely Japanese meaning during the Edo period (17th to 19th century): the cut of a sheet of washi paper folded in eight, that is, 14 × 10 cm (5.5 × 4 in). It also still refers to a book whose longest side is not more than 10 cm (4 in). The Japanese Miniature Book Association proposes an additional criterion: legibility to the naked eye.
Books measuring less than 0.95 × 0.95 mm (0.04 × 0.04) are called *micro-books*."
Text by Nicolas Codron, May 2020.

📖 MiniMa gallery library of Catherine and Kimihito Okuyama: www.librairieminima.com

• Murasaki Shikibu and Le Dit du Gengi, *text by Okuyama K., conception, design, printing and binding by Kimihito and Catherine Okuyama, 2011. Format: 7.5 × 7.6 cm (3 × 3 in), 120 g (44 lb) ivory Tropheé paper, lacquered hard cover.*
Two books, one in French and the other in English, and other leporello sides with pop-up characters inspired by old paintings.
Book awarded at the Miniature Book Society Exhibition, in Dublin (Ireland) in 2011.

📖 Miniature Book Society (MBS), United States: www.mbs.org

📖 Japanese Miniature Book Association: mamehonkyo.net

📖 Press package for the exhibition *Minuscules, les livres de très petit format à travers les siècles*, Printing Museum of Lyon, 2010: www.imprimerie.lyon.fr/static/new_imprimerie/contenu/fichiers/telch/expositions_presse/minuscule/dp_minuscule2.pdf

• *Creations of Catherine and Kimihito Okuyama at the Page(s) fair, Palais de la Femme, Paris, 2019.*

Catherine and Kimihito Okuyama are plastic artists and engravers. Their refined creations of miniature artist books have been awarded numerous prizes, in particular, in the United States, and form part of public and private collections. They exhibit their books in their quaint and small gallery MiniMa, in Paris, located in the heart of Saint-Germain-des-Prés.

Frédérique Le Lous Delpech

FRANCE

The creations of Frédérique, a book artist since he was a small child, form part of numerous collections in France and Europe. His peaceful universe transports us soothingly to his dreams.

"Artistic studies and engraving work in my studio in Rambouillet led me to the creation of unique books. They're all the story of an encounter with a text, a handmade paper, an artisan of art, a trifle collected on a beach, a detail from an Italian fresco and, especially, lovers of paper. For the book to be harmonious, you need to think about its material quality. Everything has to make sense and resonate: the subject matter, the size of the book, its shape, its binding; I make sure to take care of it. In the infinite space of possibilities that the artist book provides, creating these works one by one continues being a choice of freedom and slowness. A way of living and acting."
Frédérique Le Lous Delpech, May 2020.

"Frédérique's engraving uses nostalgic blue, gray and mauve colors, and her studio is 'that of petits papiers'. She makes her own paper. Her houses are filled with birds, tightrope walkers, poetic talismans, love messages, votive offerings. Childhood and memory envelop and unfold at the mercy of her paper castles, her 'memory weaves.'

We close her works the way we close a garden gate, her garden gate. Her artist books smell like the sea and give off the aroma of family homes. They lull the viewer into an almost melancholy daydream. She touches your heart."
Text by Marie-Christine Guyonnet,
La Librairie du Ciel, May 2020.

✉ www.atelierdespetitspapiers.com

• *104 ans séparent nos voyages, 2011- 2014.*
Digital and collagraph images
"This artist book is the artistic interpretation of the ship's log of a Breton sailor in the Far East between 1907 and 1910. It was based on my great-grandfather's writings, as well as the postcards he sent to his wife. It consists of three large thirty-page 48 x 21 cm (19 x 8) leporellos. The unfolded book is fifty meters (164 ft) long and invites the viewer to travel."

Elsa Mroziewicz

FRANCE

Elsa participates in different creative areas. She is an author and illustrator who also creates books and *paper toys*, comic books, animated films and transmedia projects. Her graphic universe is enriched by her travels and encounters in Mexico, India, Yemen and Indonesia.

She lives and works in Strasbourg. On this page she shows us a large leporello pop-up, a magnificent travelogue.

"Travel to northern Thailand. Search for the six tigers hidden in the landscapes. You can also find characters on each page: the bamboo seller, the older gentleman on a bicycle, the Akha couple, the tourist photographer and many more. Do you see them?

The scenes are inspired by the city of Chiang Rai and its streets, Phra Kaeo and Klang Wiang temples and its market. This book is my way of making a travelogue.

The leporello format enables creating a panoramic landscape with continuity. The viewer-reader can see kirigami architectures made by cutting. This reminds us that all the scenery emerges from a single sheet of paper, which enhances the *magical* effect."
Elsa Mroziewicz, December 2019.

🖴 www.elsamro.com

• 6 tigers in Thailand, *2013.*
Format: folded, 37 x 27.5 cm (15 x 11 in); unfolded, 200 cm (79 in).
Leporello cover unfolded with panoramic Thai landscape and preparatory mock-up. Children's book Cherche et trouve in kirigami, laser print paper glued on 200 g/m² (74 lb) paper, cover printed and glued on cardboard. Gouache and ink illustrations scanned and inkjet printed. Cut and assembled by hand.

J.-CH. TREBBI

"My starting point was to stage some machinery conceived at the beginning of the last century by ingenious inventors and pay homage to them. Then I proposed to Jean-Claude Planchenault the creation of the pastel illustrations.

He sent me a black-and-white photograph of a couple pedaling a strange machine, with a boy sitting between two bicycles. At first I thought it was one of his jokes. But he assured me that the photograph was of his grandparents and father in London in 1912, and that his grandfather was the inventor of that astonishing machine!"

✆ artistesdulivre.com/artistes/detailList

• La course improbable, 2015. Illustrations and pastel by Jean-Claude Planchenault.
Digital print on 300 g/m² (111 lb) Daler Rowney paper. Format: 16 x 36 cm (6 x 14 in), in sleeve.

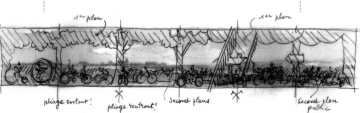

Emmanuelle Jamme

FRANCE

"My *tamponades* are to engravings what sketches are to painting: light, free-spirited works. In engraving, drawing and artist books, my work is defined around the notion of the body, the private and the every day [...] The regular drawing of real models allows me to find life in their energy and their vital force and to fix those raw moments in my memory.

In the same way, my ship's logs have accompanied for seventeen years. They're more or less my memory. They recount my daily existence, my history. I draw and write. I glue and photograph.

[...] *Streetvue* is a book that unfolds. It is placed at eye level so that the viewer can see what's going on inside thanks to the cutouts on the front. The book functions as a small theater of private life. Currently, there are four different prototypes made starting in 2012.

The fronts are drawn in lines with micron markers. Inside are linocuts glued to the pages painted the same color.

There isn't a separate cover. The book is made of 200 g/m² (74 lb) watercolor paper, glued and set together, and in some cases sewn."

Emmanuelle Jamme, February 2020.

✎ www.tamponades.com

• *Streetvue*, 2014.
Format: folded, 32 x 36 cm (13 x 14 in); unfolded, 36 cm (14 in) (height), 80 cm (32 in) (width), 40 cm (16 in) (depth).

• *Streetvue*, 2015.
Format: folded, 24 x 33 cm (13 x 14 in); unfolded, 33 cm (14 in) (height), 100 cm (32 in) (width), 40 cm (16 in) (depth).

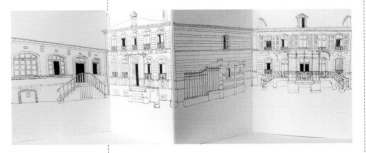

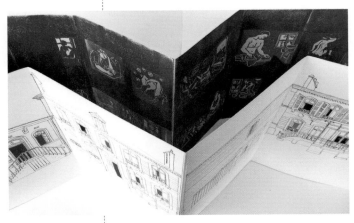

■ LEPORELLO WITH ADDED PAGES

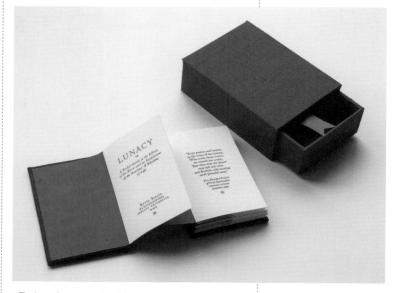

• The leporello supports the added pages.
The disassociation between support and
pages facilitates the use of different printing
techniques.

KEVIN STEELE

"The moon occupied an important place
in the cosmology of the first civilizations.
Made from observations transmitted across
the centuries through folklore, superstitions,
almanacs, biodynamics, medicine, astrology,
alchemy and witchcraft, this book of stories
in letterpress tells tales of lunar wisdom that
reached its apex with the belief that the
human spirit is a prisoner of its attraction to
this celestial body.

The structure of this work, *Lunacy*, can
be seen in two ways. First, it's possible to
read it as a traditional codex, page by page.
Later, given that the phases of the moon
are cyclical, it seemed important to me
that the reader should be able to see the
eight phases of the lunar cycle to appreciate
the whole. Also for this reason, the book
becomes a large concertina."

✏ mrkevinsteele.com

• Lunacy, 2010.
Format: folded, 6.5 x 10 x 2 cm (2.5 x 4 x 0.8
in); unfolded, 80 x 10 x 2 cm (31 x 4 x 0.8 in).
Letterpress in two colors on Hahnemühle paper
for copper, accordion binding on Arturo paper.
Cow skin covers Matchbox-style sleeve covered
with Canapetta bookcloth and ribbon. 25 copies.

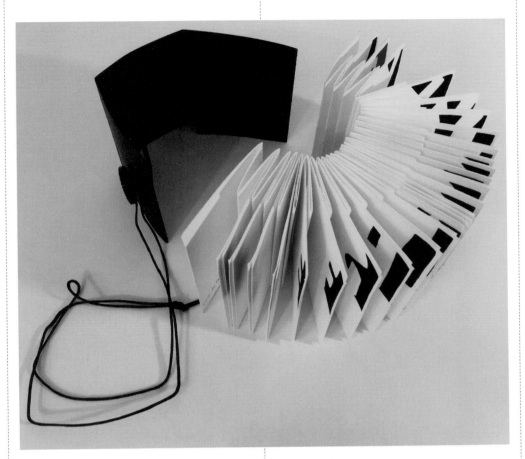

LAURENCE BUCOURT

"My project was to create an alphabet primer with the Neuland alphabet, because I love its massive and very graphic appearance. These symbols were created by the printsetter Rudolf Koch (1876-1934) in the 1920s. I chose two techniques to present them: embossing for its lightness and drawing from the counter-form for its legibility. I opted for a small-format book, with one letter per flag page, in black-and-white to respect the graphic strength of the characters. The paper is Arches MBM, adapted to embossing.

Each of the twenty-seven characters (twenty-six letters plus the symbol "et" [&]) was outlined in a 7 x 7 cm (3 x 3 in) square. These squares were later glued in sections of the book forming a one-level flag book. From the beginning, I studied the composition of each letter in each square. I chose the size of the letters, their position on the upper right angle, the drawing of their counter-forms, their placement on the upper right angle, and the drawing of their counter-forms. Then I prepared the stencils for the embossing of each letter.

I used the dry embossing technique without a press, with the help of an embossing tool, a stencil and a light table.

The counter-forms were painted with a superfine gouache brush on black velvet and China red for the symbol "et".

The accordion consists of a 210 × 7 cm (83 × 3 in) paper strip; I used four strips cut along the cluster format of my sheet. The sections are folded at 3.5 cm (1.4 in) intervals.

The cover consists of a 300 g/m² (111 lb) resistant paper dust jacket, with the flaps folded over the flyleaves. A cord tied to the sewn button on the cover allows for closing the book and protecting the pages. The book is not joined to the cover; this means it can be unfolded completely.

🖆 laurencebucourt.com

• ABC & Z, from the series Une lettre par semaine, 2018.
Format: folded, 7 x 7 x 7 cm (6 x 8 x 0.3 in); unfolded,
7 x 7 x 170 cm (16 x 10 x 8 in). Alphabet primer, flag
accordion-book, embossing and gouache. Interior: 130 g/m²
(48 lb) Ingres Arches MBM paper. Dust jacket in 300 g/m²
(111 lb) photographic paper.

■ ACCORDION BOOK
WITH CUT AND JOINED PAGES

• An example of a leporello book whose joined pages cut in semicircles provide vitality alongside the lace patterns.

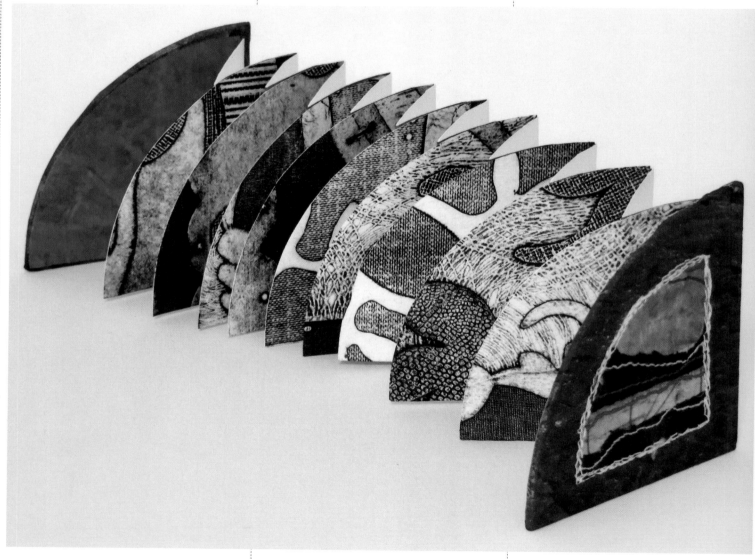

• Scallops of lace,
Annwyn Dean, 2016.
3 approx. 7 cm x 50 cm (2.6 x 20 in) copies.

ACCORDION WITH FOLDED CUT PAGES

GINA PISELLO

"When I saw that sculpture by Hedi Kyle in Cherry Moote's book *Sleight of Binding* in 2012, I immediately wanted to use it for the book. I'd just learned to fold a half crane in a map-making book. I saw the potential of this technique that allows you to fold not just into pieces of square paper. This means you can a make a crane and still have enough paper to create book pages, for example. I don't remember exactly when I decided that *Gallery Book* would be accompanied by the half cranes, but it worked out well. I took me a while to fold and cut the structure. I had to pay attention when deciding where to cut the three sides of the fold, to create a square from which the crane could be folded. It's the result of a cut and folded sheet of paper that creates a book with a dynamic shape.

I used different *vintage* maps for many reasons. To start, the birds in flight suggest travel and migration. Later, the maps are quite large, to be able to make a book from a single sheet of paper. Finally, I love maps for their colors and the overlapping pieces of text. I like the idea that the names and borders change between the past and present."

🖅 www.ginapisello.com

• Small Migrations III, 2016.
Format: 17.5 x 10 x 1.25 cm (9 x 12 x 3 in).

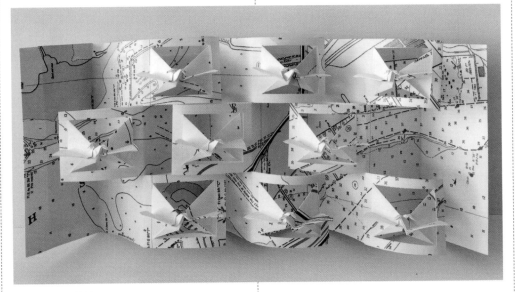

• Entanglement, 2012.
Format: 25.5 x 15 x 5 cm (9 x 12 x 3 in).

Hedi Kyle

UNITED STATES

Hedi Kyle has been making artist books for over fifty years. She was Head Conservator at the American Philosophical Society of Philadelphia, co-founder of Paper and Book Intensive (PBI), adjunct professor in the Book Arts and Printmaking program at the University of the Arts in Philadelphia, professor of book workshops in the United States and Europe and full-time artist.

She has invented an impressive amount of structures widely appropriated and modified by artists throughout the world, and her influence runs deep. Her most well-known structures are *Flag Book, the Blizzard Book, the Fishbone Fold, the Franklin Book and the Panorama Book.*

She has maintained her interest in experimentation and willingness to share her discoveries throughout her long career (more than fifty years).

In 2015, the 23 Sandy Gallery, curated by Laura Russell (Portland, Oregon), organized an international contest and exhibition titled *Hello Hedi,* for which fifty-three artists created original books based on Hedi's inventions.

Hedi Kyle is the co-author, along with her daughter Ulla Warchol, of *The Art of the Fold* (Laurence King Publishing, 2018), a superb guide that offers a broad selection of her original structures.

✎ www.artofthefold.com/hedi-kyle

• Z Words, 2005.
Format: folded, 20 x 12 x 0.5 cm; (8 x 5 x 0.2 in);
unfolded, 20 x 40 cm (8 x 16 in).
Paper Fishbone structure, 35 copies.

• Zom, 2002.
Format: folded, 5 x 12 x 5 cm; (8 x 5 x 0.2 in);
unfolded, 5 x 45 cm (8 x 16 in).
Unique panorama structure, paper and vellum,
unique copy.

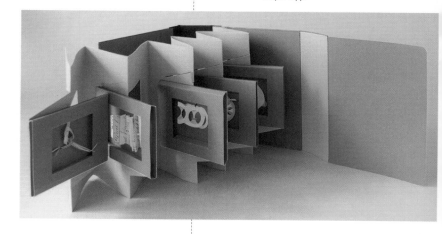

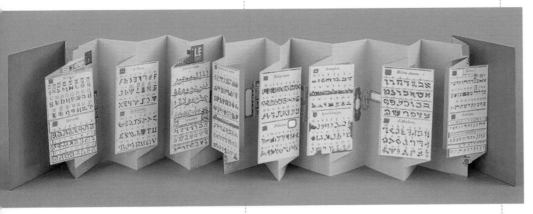

• Alphabet Panorama, 1989.
*Format: folded, 24 x 14.5 x 2.5 cm (9 x 6 x 1
in); unfolded, 24 x 1.80 m (9 in x 6 ft).
Paper and cardboard panorama structure,
unique copy, 1989.*

• Mica Flags, 2006.
*Format: folded, 23 x 11.5 x 2 cm; (8 x 23 x 0.2 in);
unfolded, 5 x 33 cm (8 x 16 in).
An unusual structure, made with sheets of Mica
paper, unique copy.*

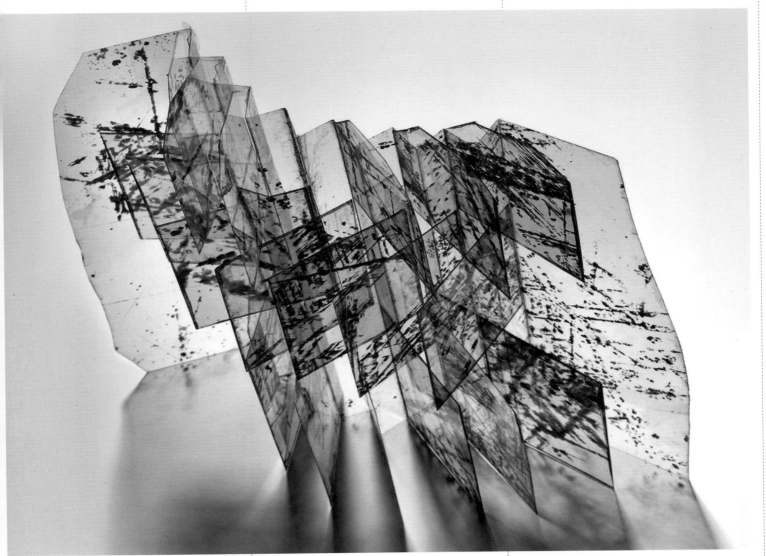

Among the many models invented by Hedi Kyle, these are the most representative.

— *Flag Book*: Hedi's first unique invention, titled *April Diary* , made in the 1970s, consists of an accordion-fold base in which small pages are glued alternatively to the right and left, creating animation. It is a kind of panoramic book with a frieze effect created by the assembly of small flags. This structure can be designed in two, three or more levels, with simple or twin loads.

— *Blizzard Book*. This book was conceived in January 1996, on a day off due to a snowstorm in Philadelphia. Kyle spent the day in her studio, experimenting with a wide variety of diagonal, straight and reverse folds using long strips of paper. As a result ,she discovered a self-binding mechanism that closes the pages from the back and creates pockets. The interest in this structure lies also in its multi-use, since the pockets can be used to store ephemeral paper collections, samples, specimens and unbound pages.

— *Panorama Book*, panorama book (also sometimes called accordion book), titled *Alphabet Panorama* and created in 1989. It is an accordion-base book with ingenious cuts that enable turning the rectangular panels, the shape of which can be changed to give them an oval or circular contour, as long as the pivot junctions remain intact.

• A to Z, 1990. A flag book structure
made of paper and cardboard, with a print run of 65 copies.
Format: folded, 31 x 16.5 x 1.25 cm; (12 x 6 x 0.5 in); unfolded; 31 x 61 cm (4 x 0.8 in).

JEAN-CHARLES TREBBI

"As artists, we're always inspired by images and sounds, by fragile stimuli. An image remains in our brain, an idea takes hold, the other disappears. Ideas collide and our brain plays tricks on us: new concept, magic brain, playful entertainment, pleasure of creating. Two of Hedi's models, whose concepts I revised, were particularly interesting to me: the *Flag Book* and the *Fishbone*. The first because it seemed apt for translating to kirigami from a single sheet of paper and several cuts. The second (called *Fishbone* because seen from above, its shape is reminiscent of the bones of a fish), because its structure allows for inserting thicker elements and transforming them by incorporating pockets and even pop-up cutouts, taking into account the spacing of the pages.

It can be adapted using the same pages or creating a diminishing structure modifying its general shape.

📧 www.artofthefold.com/hedi-kyle

📧 www.23sandy.com

📧 guildofbookworkers.org/sites/guildofbookworkers.org/files/standards/2005-Kyle_Hedi.pdf

📧 Article and flag book tutorial with step-by-step instructions in the magazine *Bonefolder*, vol. 2, no.1, Fall 2005, a digital magazine for bookbinders and book artists:
archive.org/stream/TheBonefolderE-journalForTheBookbinderAndBookArtist/BonefolderVol2No1#mode/2up

• Extension, 2016.
Format: 12.5 x 15 cm (5 x 6 in), in brown Kraft box. Leporello.
Artist book in Nostalgie de Hahnemühle paper.
Sugar Cane de Lana paper cover.

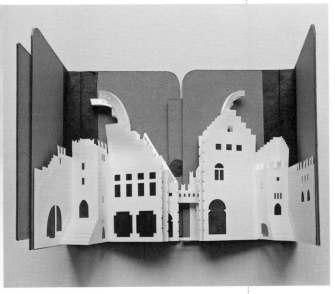

• Au bout de ma rue, je me souviens des années 60, 2017.
Format: folded, 29 x 25 cm (11 x 10 in); unfolded, 72 x 30 cm (28 x 12 in) and 25 cm (10 in). Papel Nostalgie, 190 g/m² (70 lb) Hahnemühle paper and Hermet Celloderme Bleu cardboard. "This book depicts scenes of childhood memories and nostalgia for a pleasant Parisian past. Its structure is inspired by the fishbone technique created by artist Hedi Kyle. I wanted to totally revise this foldable structure adding volume and cutout shapes."

mazes

The base of a kirigami book is a sheet of paper on which a certain number of cuts are made. These cuts form a maze. The maze book, also called instantaneous book, is simple and can be made quickly.

Highly appreciated by children and known as a "snail book", "livre meandro" or "serpent book" —like the famous Snake created by Katsumi Komagata—, the maze book has great pedagogical value, embodying play, gesture control and learning about location in three-dimensional space.

Also called a puzzle book, it allows for experimenting with the decomposition of an image that is only rebuilt when the object is unfolded completely.

Often based on an A4 format, the diagrams that we present here lend themselves to numerous geometric variations.

■ SQUARE BASE

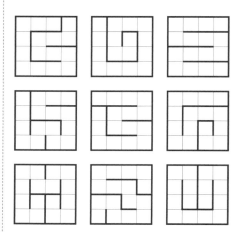

• *Proposal of nine cut diagrams, J.-Ch. Trebbi.*

• *Notes de Printemps, Brigitte Husson, 2012.*
Puzzle book on 3 x 3 cm (1 x 1 cm) square base, illustrations on both sides of an ode to "Generous Spring" in cutout.
Format: folded 8 x 8.5 cm (3 x 3.4 in); unfolded, 18 x 18.5 cm. (7 x 7.3 in) Reproduction of original format and E. looka sleeve, 2019.
✆ www.flickr.com/people/63993216@N07

• *Graines de sagesse, Frédérique Le Lous Delpech, 2016.*
Format: folded, 13 x 13 cm (5 x 5 in); unfolded, 50 x 50 cm (20 x 20 in).
"This spiral book speaks of the patience that a gardener must have toward his plot of land. Unfolding it gradually, the reader is invited to be patient also, to discover the complete harvest. Made with engraving highlighted in gouache, with text by Marie-Pierre Gaulier."
Frédérique Le Lous Delpech, May 2020.

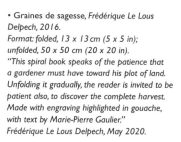

Shirley Sharoff

FRANCE

"Originally from the United States, Shirely Sharoff has lived and worked in Paris since the 1970s. The artist engraves and publishes her own books and is always seeking to expand their possibilities. Some are folded, unfolded and stand up. Sharon uses cutouts, photos, collages and engravings. Her most recent books are *Poésie de l'Univers,* with aphorisms by Aristotle, Euclid and Lavoisier; *Impermanence subtile,* with an extract from the poem *'Tri selon Tri'* by Ian Monk, member of Oulipo, and *Sur les Pas d'Erik Satie.*"

Text by the association Page)s), artist books and contemporary bibliophilia, Paris book fair, November 2019.

✏ shirleysharoff.free.fr

• Poetry of the Universe, *2012.*
Print of engravings: René Tazé studio, Paris, text composed by hand with lead sorts by Vincent Auger studio.
Measurements: 12 x 21.5 cm (5 x 8 in), three different volumes on 250 g/m² (92 lb) BFK Rives paper.
The poetry of the universe consists of three aphorisms: "The whole is greater than the sum of its parts" (Aristotle); "Parallel lines touch at infinity" (Euclid), and "Nothing is lost, nothing is created, everything is transformed" (Lavoisier).

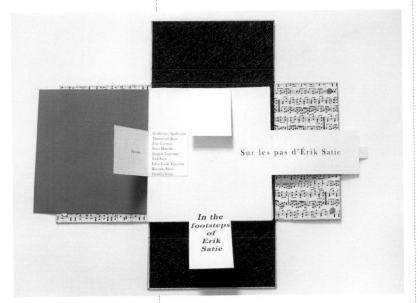

• Sur les pas d'Erik Satie, *2016.*
Cutout of windows and roof.
Measurements: 21 x 23 cm (8 x 9 in), Johannot paper. Text set by hand with lead sorts by Vincent Auger studio. Print of engravings: René Tazé studio.

Hommage à Victor Vasarely

Philippe Morlot

FRANCE

The plastic artist Phillipe Marlot is a painter, sculptor, engraver, silk screener and photographer. He has taught visual arts at the University of Lorraine. Here we see several of his creations aimed at finding a way to establish a relationship between children's literature and works of art.

"The world of children's books is one of my favorites as an artist. After publishing several works with a publishing company, I decided to create artist books for children.
They are object books designed around the concept of minimalism. I try to reduce as much as possible the size of the book by acting on all its components: page, binding, text, cover and illustration, maintaining a narration or common thread that influences the visual aspect. In a first phase, these objects are handled like a book, that is, the reader turns the pages one after the other. Later, in the second phase, the book is placed flat or in sculpture form to give it a powerful visual composition. The shape, measurements and nature of the support

are elements kept in mind from the conception of the book.
These books are also intended to facilitate the encounter with works of art such as those of François Morellet, Aurélie Nemours, Louise Bourgeois and many others.
In the technical and practical aspect, each piece begins with a direct pen, ink or pencil drawing on carbon copy paper or with a vector drawing on a computer. The resulting dies are reproduced later in a silkscreen of one or more colors.
The production is entirely natural.
These object books are artist books with limited print runs, numbered and signed, and subject to copyright deposit."
Philippe Morlot, January 2020.

✎ philippe.morlot.free.fr

Le livre-objet et l'émergence de l'enfant lecteur:
✎ www.cairn.info/revue-le-francais-aujourd-hui-2014-3-page-105.htm

• Qui tourne? *Philippe Morlot, 2019.*
Format: folded, 92 x 92 x 13 mm;
unfolded: 360 x 360 mm. Vector drawing,
monocolor silkscreen print, handmade on 270
g/m² (100 lb) white Maya Clairefontaine paper.
Numbered and signed artist book, print run of
45 copies.
"The visual road proposed can be taken at first
as a book of stories. When it is placed flat, the
visual comes into the foreground and plays with
the optical phenomenon typical of geometric
assemblages that the op art movement explored
in many aspects. This book is a special homage
to Victor Vasarely."

3	4	11	12
2	5	10	13
1	6	9	14
0	7	8	✕

• *Imposition diagram proposal,*
J.-Ch. Trebbi.
To ensure that the book, once folded, is easy
to read, the elements that make up the pages
should be adequately arranged. This operation
is called imposition. It is tested with a printer's
dummy. In this example we see a sheet of paper
on which sixteen little squares are distributed
to form a 14-page book by single-side printing.
If we want to print on both sides, only 8 pages
will be visible.

• 1/4 - 3/4, Philippe Morlot, 2016. Book in sleeve, 92 x 92 x 13 mm (4 x 4 x 0.5 in), book when flat, 360 x 360 mm (14 x 14 in). Vector drawing, two-tone silkscreen print, manual preparation on 270 g/m² (100 lb) white Maya Clairefontaine paper. Artist book, numbered and signed, print run of 45 copies.
"This book offers its own visual path of the poetic dimension of geometry. The rhythm, color and purity of the forms in their simplest expression allow for infinite combinations. With 1/4 – 3/4, I wanted to play with an elemental shape, the square made up of an assemblage of two identical triangles, to occupy the 32 pages of this minimalist book. There isn't a story. Rather there is a logic that enables creating a new proposal on each page. When placing the book flat, it provides complete balance and an abstract composition that each person can interpret in his or her own way. This book is an homage to the work of Aurélie Nemours, which I like especially for the radical quality of its plastic language."

• Suis-le, Philippe Morlot, 2016. Book in sleeve: 92 x 92 x 13 mm (4 x 4 x 0.5 in); book flat: 360 x 360 mm (14 x 14 in). Hand drawing, silkscreen print in 4 colors, manual production on 270 g/m² (100 lb) white Canson paper. Numbered and signed artist book, print run of 45 copies.

"This book was created to help the reader with the actual handling of the object. On each page is a word that forms part of a question whose answer is revealed visually when the book is placed flat. Its spiral shape corresponds to the representation of a snake. This book is also an homage to Niki de Saint-Phalle."

Kelly Seojung Lee

KOREA

Kelly lives and works in Seoul (South Korea). The artist created this model from a simple square base with a 3 × 3 grid from which she ingeniously eliminated the upper triangles to the right and the lower ones to the left. As a result, two origami bases are placed side by side yet slightly offset to allow for the creation of a *maze book* with a triangular base.

"The idea of the *Triangular Maze Fold Book* occurred to me while I was taking a course in Book Structures in college. The objective was to transform a known fold into something unique. I wanted to make a fold that was not necessarily like one in a traditional book but like a three-dimensional structure. I thought that the double-side characteristic met the objective of containing the different elements on each side, and that a surprise factor would be added when the triangular fold was placed

flat and became a single piece. I put a cord at the end of the fold so that the book could hang from the wall, where it acquires a more sculptural appearance. I want to present this fold to children as a tangible and teachable object to provide them with an interactive experience. In addition, artists can use it to present their portfolios in an original format, as, for example, I did. It's been truly incredible to see the influence this tiny fold has had on the spread of my art."
Kelly Seojung Lee, December 2019.

✎ slee58.myportfolio.com/triangular-maze-fold-book

• Triangular Maze Fold Book, 2016.
*Paperworks BC Digital White, 105 g/m²
(39 lb), simple double-sided laser print.*

■ RECTANGULAR BASE
SQUARE FOLD

• Dis Dix, Philippe Morlot, 2010.
Book in sleeve: 62 x 62 x 15 mm (2 x 2 x 0.6
in); book flat: 180 x 420 mm (14 x 14 in).
White Maya Clairefontaine paper, 270 g/m²
(100 lb), vector drawing, monotone silkscreen
print, handmade. Artist book, numbered and
signed, print run of 30 copies.
"This books revolves around complements of
ten. Each double page invites the reader to read
or say 'ten'. The form is determined by the need
of an exact number pages. In contrast to other
object books, this one has a rectangular support
subsequently cut and folded to give it a square
shape. The direction of the texts depends on
the willingness to handle the object as a book.
Unfolded, this object book is not intended to be
an autonomous plastic object."
Philippe Morlot, January 2020.

■ HOLLOW SQUARE BASE

10	9	8	7
11			6
⊠			5
1 ⓒ	2	3	4

• Fifteen cut diagram proposals.
Creation of J.-Ch. Trebbi.

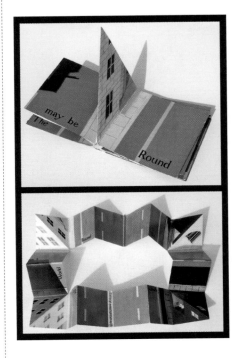

• Intersection, Ken Leslie.
Format: folded, 7.5 x 7.5 x 1 cm; (8 x 44 x 0.2 in);
unfolded, 5 x 29 cm (8 x 16 in).
A rectangular bull whose special quality resides in
the folded angles.

■ TRIANGULAR BASE HOLLOW CENTER

Martine Gautier

FRANCE

Martine makes her own paper. This former teacher, alchemist, even a bit of a sorceress in her adventures as a researcher, and also a smuggler of wisdom, loves to experiment, combining the fibers of sometimes unusual plants such as milkweed, common wild oat, amadou and Phragmites australis.

"In a world buried under useless papers, where books are being replaced by tablets, where access to knowledge has dematerialized, why make paper? Without a doubt, because it's crucial to reestablish a connection with nature and to remember that nature is what nurtures and inspires us since the dawn of time. It's about returning enchantment to our world by giving new meaning to the futile or insignificant, to invite people to dream, to travel through time and space and recover the experience and knowledge of the ancients.
It's about being open to encounters, to exchanges, to sharing, to rediscovering the primordial meaning of writing: communication."
Martine Gautier, December 2019.

🕮 lokta.fr

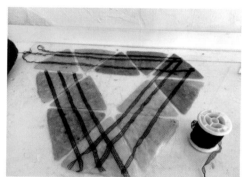

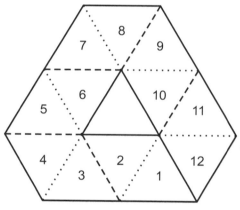

• Livre triangulaire, *2019.*
Format: folded, 10 cm (4 in) sideways and 3.5 cm (1 in) thick; unfolded, 33 x 33 cm (13 in).
"A triangular base maze book made from hemp and 4,500 year-old dead oak- a morta Brière - fiber. Nüshu signs (special Chinese writing reserved exclusively for women which only they know how to read) associated with Breton lace."

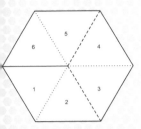

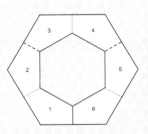

• Large hexagon and small center.

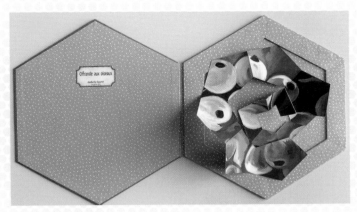

• Offrande aux oiseaux, Isabelle Faivre, 2020.
Format: painting, 26 x 22.5 cm (10 x 9 in);
in 30 x 34 x 1 cm (12 x 13 x 0.4 in) sleeve.
Painting unharvested red currants that become a
gift for birds.

• Small hexagon, triangular fold.

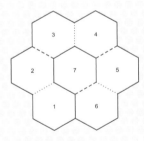

• Small spiral hexagon.

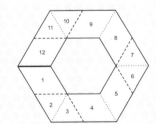

• Large hexagon,
diamond-shaped pages.

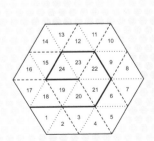

• Large spiral hexagon.

• Hexatonic Prime, 2016.
Six 13 x 15 cm (5 x 6 in) hexagonal panels.

Thomas Parker

UNITED STATES

Thomas Parker Williams lives and works in Philadelphia. He makes artist books and engraves and paints. Some of his books contain an audio element - music or sound piece - which he composes, performs and records himself. His books are part of many public and private collections.

"For twenty years I've painted using a variety of mediums to explore a wide array of themes. I began to make books related to a series I was working on when I discovered that making artist books suited my methods, because it's an activity that grants more freedom in terms of subject matter and form than painting. I'm also a musician, and the book format allows me to add a musical element to the work as a whole.

The initial idea for *Hexatonic Prime* is to create a musical composition in two parts using a hexatonic mode whose notes correspond to the six prime numbers between two and thirteen.
I chose a hexagon for the structure. The colors were printed in linocut. The musical scales on the back of the panels were silkscreened. The colors represent my perception of the different modes."
Thomas Parker, November 2019.

✐ www.thomasparkerwilliams.com

■ HEXAGON, VARIATION

• Hawksted Critters, *Ed Hutchins, 2020.*
From an alveolar weave in the form of a
beehive, the artist takes us on an astonishing
journey in this twenty-four page maze book.

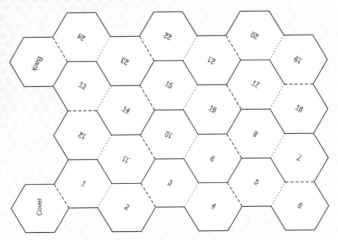

■ OCTAGON BASE
8 TRAPEZOIDAL PAGES
HOLLOW CENTER

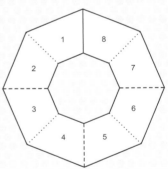

• Octo Novo, *J.-Ch. Trebbi, 2019.*
Format: folded, 16 x 24 cm (6 x 9 in);
unfolded, 58 x 58 cm (23 x 23 in) forming
an octagon.
Each page of this model is unique and
represents esoteric symbols and expressions
made with random chemical etching. On
Nostalgie Hahnemühle white paper, and
watercolor Gerstaecker, Curious skin Li rose de
Arjowiggins paper background.

Ken Leslie

UNITED STATES

"I live in Vermont, a region its inhabitants think of as Nordic. For twenty years, I've been painting and making artist books about the Earth and our place in space, literally and philosophically. This interest led me to the North Pole, where the presence (and absence) of the sun alters the inclination of the Earth toward or away from it. I've done more than a dozen projects in the Arctic - in Iceland, in northern Alaska, in Greenland, in northern Finland and in Norway.

I invented a structure, the toroide book, which allows me to follow the movement of time through space. This donut folded accordion style creates images (and sometimes texts) that move in a complete circle, often forming a panoramic landscape. I use the fan structure of pages to measure the time, hours, days, weeks and even years in some books. Painting, the book, the art of the *performance*, time and place are at the heart of each work. These books become quite voluminous and can be exhibited as paintings when unfolded completely. Generally, they have a diameter of 130 cm (51 in), but I also have created works three times as big."

Ken Leslie, January 2020.

• Iqaluit summer, Iqaluit (Nunavut Canada),
2007.

• Akureyri summer, Akureyri (Iceland), 1999.

"A few words about the structure of my toroide book might help to understand it. All the pages are the same size except the first and last, which function as front and back covers. For this reason, they are slightly larger to accommodate the accordion fold. There is also a thin piece of supplementary tape fitted to the circumference that serves as the book's spine. [...] A secondary advantage is being able to transport large paintings in a small suitcase. This allows me to share the collection of arctic cycle books with each of the communities involved. [...] On a large-format printer, I publish an edition of the book and in each place disseminate it among the people who participated in the project, as well as in schools, libraries and museums."

Ken Leslie, extracts from Book Arts, *Canada 2014, vol. 5, no. 2.*

✎ www.kenleslie.net

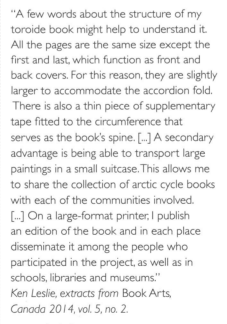

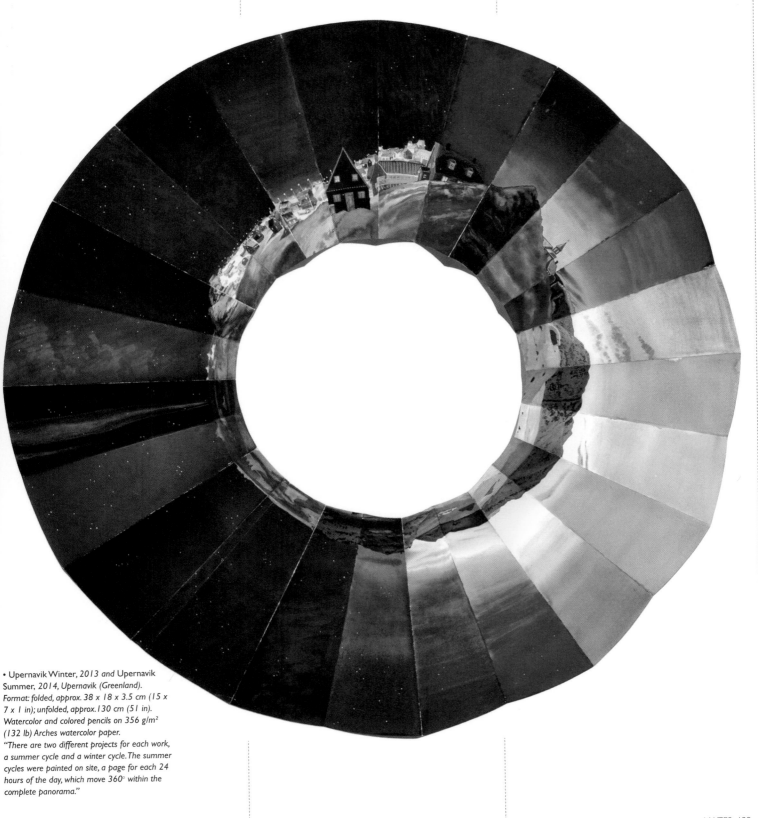

• Upernavik Winter, *2013 and* Upernavik
Summer, *2014, Upernavik (Greenland).*
Format: folded, approx. 38 x 18 x 3.5 cm (15 x
7 x 1 in); unfolded, approx. 130 cm (51 in).
Watercolor and colored pencils on 356 g/m²
(132 lb) Arches watercolor paper.
"There are two different projects for each work,
a summer cycle and a winter cycle. The summer
cycles were painted on site, a page for each 24
hours of the day, which move 360° within the
complete panorama."

• Natural Un-Natural, *Thomas Parker, 2015.*
"Painted book, with a double accordion structure of twelve two-sided panels. Twenty-four images in all, six of the panels can be fixed at the same time. The panels, painted with dry oil pigments on paper, evoke the theme of climate change."

🖥 www.thomasparkerwilliams.com

• La PpP, *Philippe Morlot, 2017.*
Format: folded, 70 x 92 x 20 mm (3 x 4 x 0.8 in); unfolded, diameter 370 mm (14.5 in). 270 g/m² (100 lb) white Maya Clairefontaine paper. Vector drawing, silkscreen print in three colors, handmade. Artist book, numbered and signed, print run of 45 copies.
"In the PpP, I tried, in my own way, to tell the story of the princess and the pea by Hans Christian Andersen.. I decided to use the circular shape to approximate the shape of a pea. I worked with the page makeup and the form of the pages for a classic reading (turning the pages) and, later, with an unfolded leporello to reveal, when placed flat, the object that allows the story to be told, i.e., the pea. The written story ends with this sentence and with the pea exposed in the cabinet of art treasures - hence my wanting to put this round shape forward. On the back of the book sleeve is a stylized representation of the characters to make it easier to read the story."

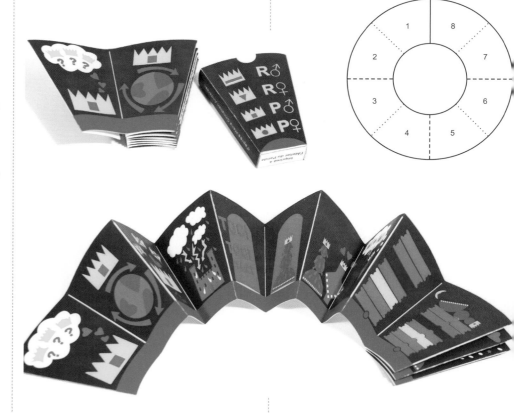

■ HEXAGON BASE
CURVED PAGES

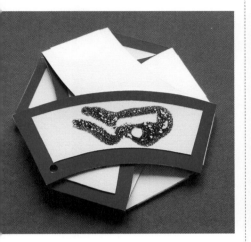

• Octa kurba, *J.-Ch. Trebbi, 2019.*
Format: folded 16 x 16 x 0.5 cm (6 x 6 x 0.2
in); unfolded, 98 cm (39 in). Unique copy.
"I wanted to make an accordion book with
round pages. For this, I joined curved strips to
hexagon sides to obtain a kind of leporello to be
read vertically which, unfolded, presents highly
graphical waves. When the book is folded, the
silhouette of the hexagon reappears."

■ CIRCULAR BASE
POP-UP BOOK

Kevin Steele

UNITED STATES

"*The Deep* is an homage to folklore and maritime traditions developed over centuries of nautical exploration. The ocean, which remains immense and mysterious even today, was even more fascinating and terrifying for sailors at a time when sea travel meant being very far away from everything, in often unchartered waters and dangerous regions.

The Deep is a circular accordion-style pop-up book that unfolds like a giant eight-point wind rose. The compass, without a doubt the sailor's most precious instrument, makes not only navigation possible but also guarantees the return home, because it removes the danger of becoming lost at sea. For me, it was important that the structure of this book refer to the content.

Given that the wind rose is an important symbol and my book was intended to be like a navigation guide, it seemed appropriate to model it after the shape of this important instrument.

The conception of the structure presented several challenges. The book had to be big enough to contain ten thousand words. Yet it also needed to be folded compactly for safe storage and transport. It had to

be circular but have points that unfolded in eight directions. My starting point was a simple circle. I studied the way to develop this shape and the mechanisms that could be added to create the details of the wind rose as the book evolved.

The process required multiple paper models and countless adjustments; so progress was slow. After defining the most accurate conceptualization, I created lines of numerical dies to obtain the exact measurements and angles for all the pieces. With a good printer's dummy, I could then begin to situate the text and images on the cut lines."

Kevin Steele, February 2020.

✉ mrkevinsteele.com

• The Deep, *Kevin Steele, 2012.*
Format: unfolded, 1.63 m x 1.70 m (5.4 x 5.6 ft)
box: 29 x 46 x 14 cm (9 x 12 x 3 in).
Print run: 10 copies
The text and images were ink jet printed on Beckett Expression paper.
The pop-ups were cut by hand and then mounted in wrapped cardboard on Canapetta paper. The work is kept in a storage box in the shape of one of the points of the rose and which also contains a signed and numbered colophon.

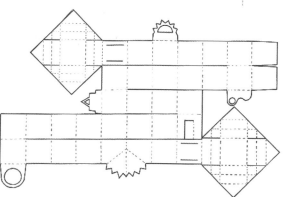

• The Magic of the Mystery Box, *Edward Hutchins, 1996.*

"*Last year in the Anchorage Musuem of History and Art, David Edlefsen asked me to come up with an idea for the catalog of an artist box exhibition. I suggested that the catalog itself should be a box (how could it be otherwise?), and David loved the idea.*

The catalog is a 61 x 91.5 cm (24 x 36 in) sheet of paper printed in four colors on one side and one color on the other. The die-cut technique was used to cut it into a continuous sheet that folds into a fifty-six page catalog with a pop-up, a door, several sides and a box in two parts to hold it.

I designed the structure combining Scott McCarney's bustofredon format with Keith Smith's book-and-box.

Barbara Mauriello came up with the idea for the covers of the boxes and Julia Decker handled the production layout in Alaska. Ron Qowen wrote the text, structuring it so that each paragraph occupies a page. It was one of those projects in which everything seemed to be against us, but in the end it turned out to be a true success. I'm happy I was able to participate in it."

Edward Hutchins, 1996.

Ed Hutchins

UNITED STATES

Ed Hutchins has had an amazing career. Do you know that over the course of forty years, this modest man has published more than one hundred and fifty artist books and hundreds of ephemeral pieces? And that he has also led numerous teaching workshops, mostly in the United States and Mexico, and organized four book festivals, always with the desire to share his knowledge of and experiences with innovative book structures?

The philosophy of Ed Hutchins is to make books in *bookmaking guerrilla* style, where "anyone can make a book because everybody has a story to tell." Books are made with things we have at hand and require simple skills within the reach of everyone.

The books that Hutchins creates usually do not resemble others. They are books made from a single sheet of folded paper, or tunnel books that allow the reader to see through them, or flexagons in which each page is folded over itself to create a new page.

Anne Anninger, Houghton Library, Philip Hofer, conservator of Printing & Graphic Arts, collected Hutchins' books for the library at Harvard and said: "The philosophy of Hutchins' books can be summed up as follows: start by thinking deeply about the human species, express your profound concern for it in a few simple words, add

evocative images, present it all is a unique, humorous and expressive structure that requires years of experience but also the irreverence of youth. Impossible you say? Not for Ed Hutchins."

🖙 www.artistbooks.com

🖙 edhutchins.com/guerilla-bookmaking.html

🖙 edhutchins.com/how-i-got-to-be-a-book-artist.html

🖙 byopiapressdotcom1.files.wordpress.com/2018/09/bookdynamics_thebookfolder.pdf

🖙 www.worddisk.com/wiki/Edward_H._Hutchins

"We tend to see books as pieces of paper folded in two and joined in one way or another between two cardboard covers. But there are many other possibilities."
Ed Hutchins

Tunnel books

A magical universe

Completely integrated into animated books or system books, tunnel books have inspired research in diverse and innovative structures. Also called dioramas, optical panoramas, image boxes and *peep-shows*, this form of miniature theater presents scenes interconnected by bellows. Yet, the interest in this object lies in its being able to be folded, which makes storing it easier.

"Tunnel books transform two-dimensional images into a three-dimensional world. They take us out of one world and immerse us in another. 'The entire idea of tunnel books, explains Joe Freedman, is to raise your eyes to the Judas hole (the peephole), enter and become part of the interior landscape.'

Peep shows and tunnel shows are an original form of immersion technology.
The *peep show* was the virtual reality of the 19th century, and tunnel books are the paper equivalent of today's interactive game technology." Ed Hutchins, *Calling on Tunnel Books, 10 Years Later, 2012.*

In Europe, in the 17th century, *showmen* would go from town to town presenting different historical or religious scenes in optical boxes which they carried on their backs. The box had a peephole and, often, a change of view mechanism, and the lens was its most precious element. In Japan, during the Edo period (1603-1868), *Tatebanko*, or paper dioramas appeared. These were objects that represented monuments, elements of Kabuki theater and historical scenes. Improvements in printing techniques in the 18th century enabled the publication of game books for domestic use. Between 1740 and 1770, the printer Martin Engelbrecht presented an astonishing catalog of *peep shows* of between six and eight panels.

Starting in 1825, *optiques* appeared in France. These were small paper structures with between four and six scenes such as, for example, the *Optique militaire avec changement de tableaux* (publisher Mallez Ainé, Paris,) or the *Cathédrale de Reims*, *La Fête de Longchamp* and *Le Palais Royal*. These *peep shows* were often created to celebrate important events such as the Great Exhibition in London and the opening of the tunnel under the Thames in 1843, which, according to Carol Barton, was the origin of the expression *"tunnel book"*. The creations of this period usually had three front holes with three different points of view.

• The great exhibition of all nations, telescopic view of the ceremony of her majesty opening, *published by Charles Auguste Lane, illustrated by Rawlins, 1851, reprinted by Antiquus viejos ingenios.*
View of the Crystal Palace made for the opening ceremony held by Queen Victoria at the first universal exposition.

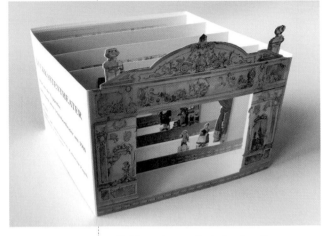

• Guckkastentheater, *reproduction of an old theatre book (c. 1900). Doll and Toy Museum, Puppen & Spielzeugmuseum Katharina Engels, Rothenburg, (Germany).*

• Gaiarama, The unfolding adventures in The Rain Forest, *edited by White Eagle, 1992-1995.*

🕮 www.sarabande.com

🕮 Hutchins Ed, *Exploring Tunnel Books*, 1994.

🕮 www.philobiblon.com/gbwarticle/hutchins1.PDF

🕮 Hutchins Ed, *Calling on Tunnel Books, 10 Years Later*. Movable Stationery 08/12, volume 20, No. 3.

🕮 Huebsch Rand, *Tunnel Book, A Theatrical Structure*, New York, Movable Stationary, vol.9, 2001.

🕮 Balzer Richard, *Peep-shows, A Visual History*, Harry N. Abrams, Inc., New York,1998.

🕮 www.dickbalzer.com

🕮 Hyde Ralph, *Paper Peep-shows, The Jacqueline and Jonathan Gestetner Collection, Antique collectors'*, Club Ltd, Woodbridge, Suffolk, England, 2015.

🕮 Huhtamo Erkki, *The Pleasures of the Peephole: An Archaeological Exploration of Peep Media, Book of Imaginary Media: Excavating the Dream of the Ultimate Communication Medium,* Eric Kluitenberg, Nai, Rotterdam, 2004.

🕮 Desmonds Clémentine, *restauration de livres tunnels anciens*, see article devoted to the subject on the French reference webpage about animated books: www.livresanimes.com/actualites actu1806larestaurationdunlivretunnel.htm

• Patente Pihlström, 1887. *"My invention consists of a foldable and extendable device made up of sheets with flat and rigid ends joined by flexible walls. The sheet on one end offers a view with a central perspective and the sheet at the other end has a peephole..."*

Ten systems of structure composition and positioning of the bellows:

• 1: Side bellows with drawings of the scenes attached by intermittent clamping.
2: Accordion fold bellows. The scenes have side tabs.
3: M-shaped bellows inserts between the scenes.
4: C-shaped bellows fastened with rivets oriented toward the interior or the exterior.
5: The scenes have side flaps with cuts for the lace (see J.-C. Planchenault model).
6: The scenes and bellows are formed by two symmetrical strips arranged at points on the central part.
7: The scenes have partitions cut in the central window and that unfold sideways; the form of the window, in this case, is fixed (Carol Barton model), horizontal or vertical bellows.
8: The bellows folded in an accordion strip has cuts that receive the overhanging tabs of the scenes (see J-Ch. Trebbi model).
9: The scenes have small side tabs; the entire model folds sideways.
10: The scenes and bellows are made with a single accordion fold strip.

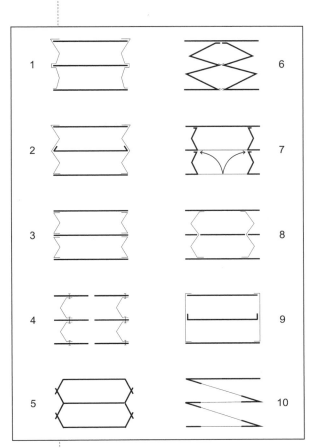

Types of tunnel books

"The tunnel book contains an inherent paradox: it is a three-dimensional structure made up of two-dimensional elements. This dichotomy gives its format a special visual logic that allows for stylization. The perspective can be manipulated and forced like a museum diorama."

The structure, the skeleton of a classic tunnel *book*, is made up of scenes arranged one after the other and laterally joined by two paper strips folded accordion style.

It is the traditional model invented when the tunnel under the Thames was built in London.

There are different variations based on the shape and size of the bellows or fastening retractors and in its modes of assembly. Often they are glued or fit together. Sometimes the bellows are joined with a thin piece of tape, flat cords or rivets. Several artists, such as Roy Doty, Ed Hutchins and Paul Johnson, have made tunnel books from a single folded sheet of paper with cuts.

There is no cover in the traditional models. For protection, a simple side cover or, infrequently, a double cover is included in modern structures.

* Rand Huebsch, *Tunnel Book: A Theatrical Structure, New York City, Movable Stationary, vol.9, 2001.*

• *Les 3 Dumas, Béatrice Coron, 2017. Poem by James Noël. Format: 14 x 14 cm (5.5 x 5.5 in).*

• Paris, *1830. Ed Hutchins Collection.*

Some tunnel books have a fixed structure. The scene designs are supported by horizontal rods (like bolts with screws) situated at the four angles of the scene designs and small separation tubes interspersed to keep the scenes at equal or unequal distances.

"The creation of a tunnel book is more complicated than it appears at first. [...] The ideal structure of one should have three different thicknesses. The front and back covers must be especially thick and solid to resist repeated openings and closings and to ensure they don't bend in the process. The central panels need to be thick enough to remain rigid when the book is open. The side hinges must be thin, solid and flexible so that the book is as flat and thin as possible when folded." *Ed Hutchins*

Peepholes

The peepholes situated on the front scene can have many forms: round simple classic viewfinder or oval, double... In his creation *Grandma's Closet*, Ed Hutchins made a peephole in the shape of a keyhole to reveal the inside of the closet that holds his grandmother's treasures.

"The openings in the covers of tunnel books range from small Judas holes to very wide squares. The eye needs a certain distance to focus, and the smaller the opening on the cover the more distance is required between it and the first panel. Unless the dimensions of the peephole are large, more space is needed from the cover to the first panel than between the other panels. Even the first visualization boxes had this optical imperative in mind."
Ed Hutchins

• Grandma's Closet, *Ed Hutchins, 1991. Peepholes are usually circular, at times oval, but all shapes are acceptable. For this creation, the artist made a viewfinder in the shape of a keyhole to enable seeing the inside of the closet containing his grandmother's treasures.*

• Paris, 1830, Ed Hutchins Collection.
In it is classic position, the peephole is usually in the center of the main page. Less frequently, some modes have two or three peepholes, mainly in cases with a superimposed double structure.

• Das Rheinthal, la vallée du Rhin de Bingen jusqu'à Lurley, ca. 1930.
Kristine Suhr Collection.

■ FRONTAL UNFOLDING WITH HORIZONTAL BELLOWS

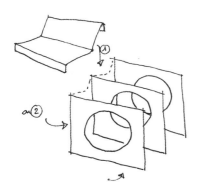

• The folded strip that forms the bellows is fixed horizontally to the upper and lower part of the scenes.

• Thames tunnel, *1851,*
Ed Hutchins Collection.

• Das Rheinthal, la vallée du Rhin de Bingen jusqu'à Lurley, *ca. 1930.*
Kristine Suhr collection

• Charles Trenet, Fais ta vie, *Gérard Lo Monaco, 1995.*
Album sleeve

■ FRONTAL UNFOLDING
WITH VERTICAL BELLOWS

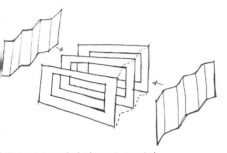

• The strip is attached sideways in a vertical position to the right and left of the scenes; the joining of the tabs in the bellows provides a somewhat soft articulation.

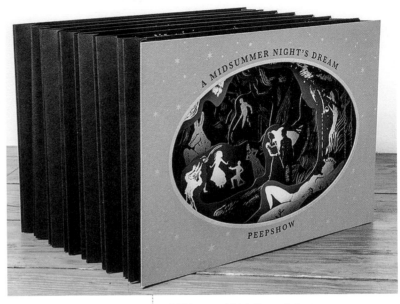

• A Midsummer Night's Dream, A silent book, *Daniele Catalli, 2014. PiriPiri Atelier, Turin, Italy. J.-Ch. Trebbi Collection*

• The Tunnel Calamity, *Edward Gorey, G. P. Putnam's Sons publishing, New York, 1984.*

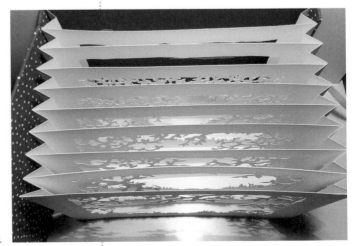

• Sérénité, *Patricia Cavrois, 2009.*

■ LATERAL UNFOLDING

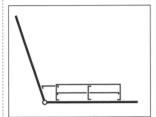

• Peeps into Fairy Land, *Ernest Nister, 1895.*
*The scene designs are attached in the right (or
left) part of the book. One or two tabs on the
left (or right) part enable lifting the book when
it is opened.*
Françoise Sagan media collection,
Jeunesse Heure Joyeuse endowment fund.

■ VERTICAL UNFOLDING

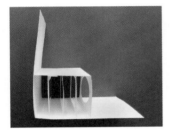

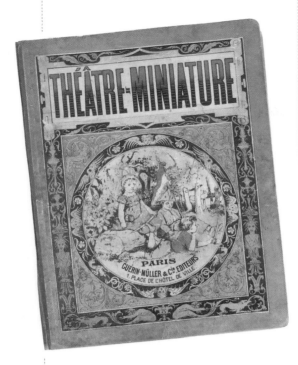

• Théâtre-miniature, Paris, Guérin-Müller et Cie éditeurs, (ca.1880).
Pop-up model raised by placing a piece of tape in the upper part. The designs are inserted inside an encircling form that is folded; the juncture of the high and low tabs provides rigidness to the fold.
The support is achieved through foldable tabs situated in the background.
There is a box variation of this structure, for example, in La Grande Ménagerie by A. Capendud, consisting of six panels, published in Paris in 1885.
Françoise Sagan media collection, Jeunesse Heure Joyeuse endowment fund.

■ BOX SYSTEM

This book, which was first published in 1878, by J.F. Schreiber of Esslingen, Germany, contains four scenes on stage: one from Little Red Riding Hood, one from Hansel and Grethel, one showing the nativity scene, and the final one with a family around the tree on Christmas Eve. Any one of these could be acted with your own family or friends.

• The Children's Theatre, *Franz Bonn, Kestrel Books, 1978 (reproduction of a 1978 work published by J.F. Schreiber, Esslingen, Germany). Original system conceived for box and with different assembled scenes.*

Set up the stage, bring out the gear
For Christmas-time is getting near.
Jackets and breeches, skirts and smocks
Come from the nursery dressing-box.
And everybody gathers round
To act a scene in shape and sound:
Fanny and Fido in the wood
Imitate Red Riding Hood,
While down below the Fauntleroys
Play minuets – a dreadful noise.

■ BOX SYSTEM
PODIUM VARIATION

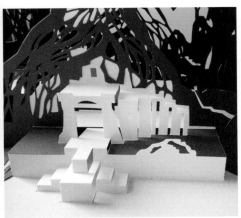

• *Racines, J.-Ch. Trebbi, 2017.*
Format: folded, 30 x 42 cm (5 x 5 in);
unfolded, 42 x 60 cm (20 x 20 in).
Large pop-up book made for the 3rd book fair and its art
professions, organized by Anima Libri in Montreuil Bellay.

■ BUILDING ELEMENTS

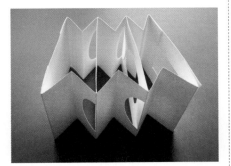

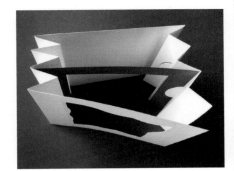

• *Tabs cut in the bellows*

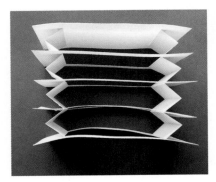

• *Bellows cut in a window, Carol Barton model.*

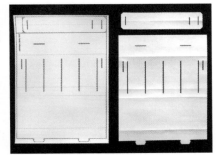

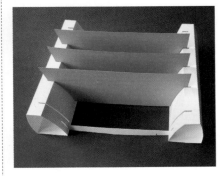

• *A useful practice for making tunnel books is
the preparation support of the scenes. There
are several possible systems: a large rectangular
wood or compact foam support in which slots
are made at regular intervals; an old CD-ROM
support or even, as Rand Huebsch proposes, an
appropriately adapted metal hanger.*

*Here is a model I came up with for a tunnel
book workshop with the enthusiastic team
from Médiathèque d'Anglet. Easy to make and
position, it enables situating the scenes so that
you can check their definitive appearance before
the final assembly.*

■ SINGLE PIECE SYSTEM
VARIATION A

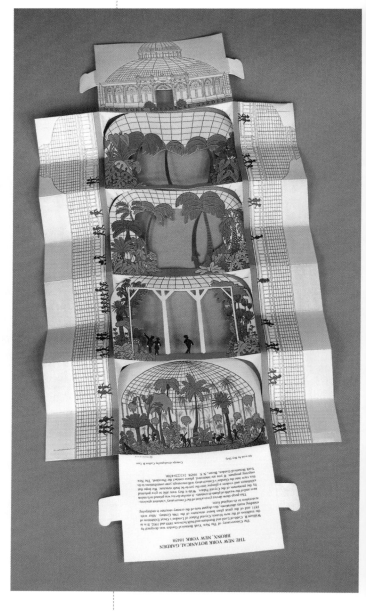

• The New York Botanical Garden, *1977, designed by Carlton B. Lees, illustrated by Roy Doty and made by Ed Hutchins.*
The advantage of this ingenious system lies in its being made from a single sheet of cut and folded paper. The set of scenes is flat. For this reason, it is necessary to imagine the assembly and organize the scenes.

• Lunch pattern, *Ed Hutchins, 1996.*

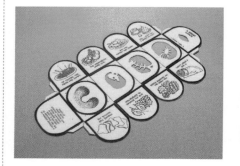

■ SINGLE PIECE SYSTEM
VARIATION B

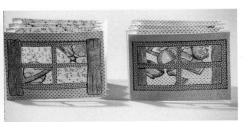

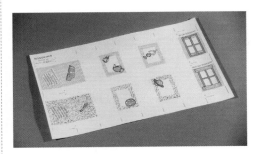

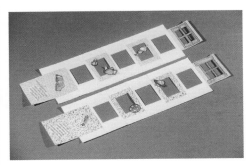

• In my window, *Ed Hutchins, 1994.*
The structures of tunnel books are one of Ed's passions. He has a beautiful collection of this type of book. The artist has designed and made forty-one tunnel books, all very different from each other. Here we see one of his creations, dating from 1994. Imagined as always for a single sheet of paper, in this case, it includes the semi-bellows that must be glued to give it form.
⊜ www.artistbooks.com

■ VERTICAL BELLOWS FIT TOGETHER

Jean-Claude Planchenault

FRANCE

Jean-Claude Planchenault is an architect, model maker and painter. He lives and works in Paris, in Levallois-Perret. In the course of his travels, his sketch book replaces his camera. He has exhibited his pastels in France and Peru, his wife's native land and whose landscapes, architecture and people have often inspired his work.

His passion for dioramas has its origins in a old puppet theater in his parents' library. For twenty years, he has made bound tunnel books according to his own formulation. They depict, among other things, Parisian landscapes, perspectives of the city and scenes from the Middle Ages with hidden parts to be searched for.

Jean-Claude Planchenault made and patented an ingenious system with bellows of decreasing size inserted in the scene designs with notches that allow them to be fit together.

✆ www.artistesdulivre.com/artistes/detailList.php?ID=41

• Exhibition of works by Jean-Claude Planchenault in La Sévrienne des Arts, 2019.

• Le passage des Panoramas, 2003, La galerie Colbert, 2015, Le passage du Grand-Cerf, J.-C. Planchenault, 2017. Format: 9.5 x 13.5 cm (4 x 0.8 in).

■ BELLOWS WITH SIDE BEARER STRIPS

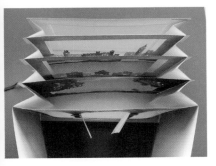

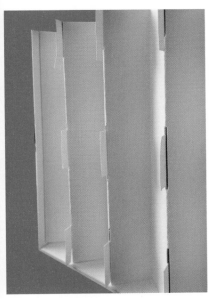

• *Souvenirs d'Italie, J.-Ch. Trebbi, 2011.*
The scene designs have tabs that fit together in
the bellows with a closing system. To stabilize the
open book, two tabs situated in the lower part
of the main scene fit together in a horizontal
slot on the cover.

■ BEARER BELLOWS

• *De Chartres à Paris, J.-Ch. Trebbi, 2015.*
Format: folded, 35 x 26.5 x 2 cm (14 x 10 x
0.8.in); unfolded: 141 x 26.5 x 13.5 cm (9 x
12 x 3 in).
Materials: bamboo and brown Kraft papers.
Manually cut pop-up tunnel book, illustrated
with documents about Western railways.
"For the exhibition 'Délires de Livres' organized
in 2015 by Chantal and Paul Leibenguth, of
Am'Arts, around the theme 'If we become
allies...', I imagined this large manually cut
animated pop-up book about Western railways."
The curved bearer strips have slots above and
below in which the different scenario designs
are inserted. This tunnel book system has a dual
view, front and side.

🖢 www.am-arts.com

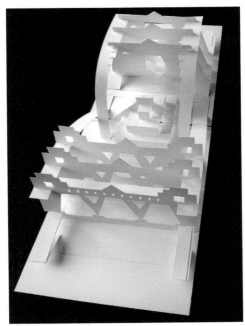

• Preparatory study prototype.

■ DOUBLE TUNNEL

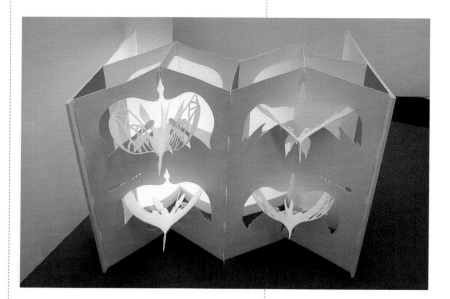

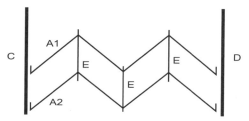

• Désir d'envol, J.-Ch. Trebbi, 2013.
Black sleeve: 33 x 47 cm (4 x 0.8 in). Unique copy.
This leporello consisting of two parallel beds supported by retractors allows for lateral movement; the covers unfold in parallel fashion. A special large format double tunnel book concept in pop-up form that lights up in front of a window. Bamboo paper against a translucent sulphurized white background and red side walls reflected in the birds' wings. Mini pop-up book on front cover.

■ PANORAMA STRUCTURE

• *These forms are similar to tunnel books, but the position of the scenes is different. They are joined side by side forming a leporello panorama with two or three multilayer scenes interconnected by simple separation systems consisting of folded strips or with fit shapes with cuts for inserting the scenes. This last system functions as a series of hinges and provides more softness in the lateral unfolding.*

The Apertolo model provides a more panoramic opening than the previous one, with scenes on three levels at the ends of different lengths. Some tips: pay attention to the size of the covers, which need to be enveloping, and keep in mind the refolding of the scenes. Make a diagram to scale to define the diminishing lengths of the scenes.

Two solutions for possible variations in the elaboration of the retractors:
– they can be partial and made up of a folded strip with two tabs glued on the scenes;
– they can be made with strips with cuts that fit together in the scenes, a solution that offers more softness in the refolding.

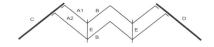

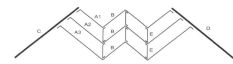

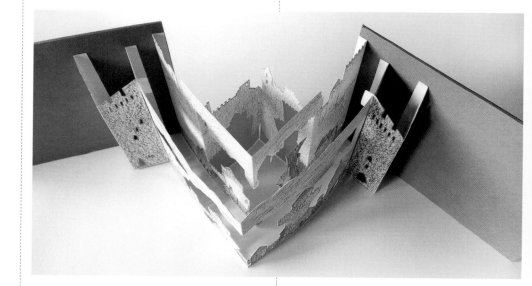

TUNNEL
SIDE EXTENSIONS

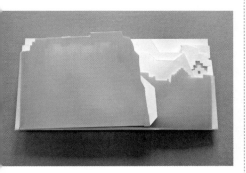

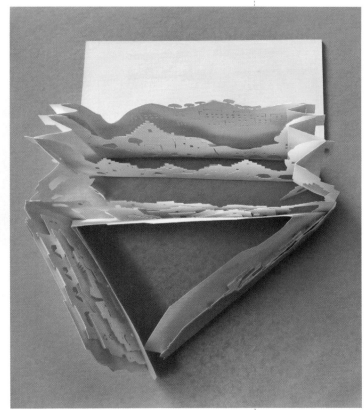

• Matera, une cité dans la roche, J.-Ch. Trebbi, 2014. Format: folded, 15.5 x 31 cm (6 x 12 in); unfolded: approx 40 x 64 cm (16 x 25 in). Foldable cover that forms the base; brown Kraft sleeve.

"This pop-up theater book has two side extensions that unfold onto themselves, thereby enhancing the panoramic view. With this book, I wanted to pay homage to that troglodyte city of art and history in southern Italy, the pearl of Basilcate, listed as a UNESCO World Heritage Site and chosen as the European culture capital 2019."

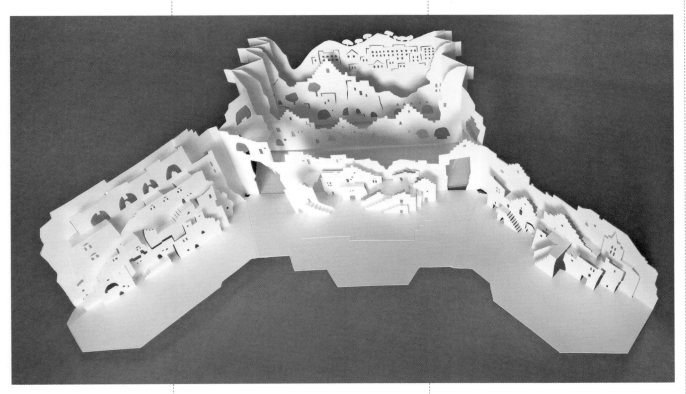

Carousel books

This is another type of miniature theater book, sometimes called *"star book"* or also "accordion carousel book" because it is a sophisticated variation of the accordion book. It consists of four, five, six and up to seven scenes or panels in relief. It opens 360° and the whole forms an object that reveals all the scenes like a small theater. This system is often used in toy books in the form of a doll's house or forts.

The generic term is *carousel book*, but Paul Johnson points out the structural difference between this book and the star book. There is, in fact, an important dissimilarity in terms of structure. In the carousel book, the scenes are made up of several layers of different sizes; in the star book the layers are arranged differently thanks to a folded base and pop-up structures usually attached to the side walls.

✏ Paul Johnson, "Star Vs. Carousel", *Movable Stationery*, vol. 28 no.2, June 2020.

• Ali Baba & the forty thieves, a peep-show book, *Houghton Mifflin Co, 1950. J-.Ch. Trebbi Collection*

• Tell me why, *Steve Warren and Ed Hutchins, 2000. Mini theater book with scenes in relief. Unfolded format: 7.3 x 6.7 cm (2.9 x 2.7 in). This model, which Ed made from a single sheet of paper and published in his book Book Dynamics!, allows for creating a mini carousel book with four scenes.*

Ali Baba e i 40 ladroni, *Theater Book*, Hoepli,
Milan, 1940. Format: folded, 23 x 23 cm (9 x 9 in);
unfolded: approx. 50 cm (20 in) diameter.
Pietro Franchi Collection

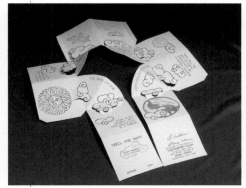

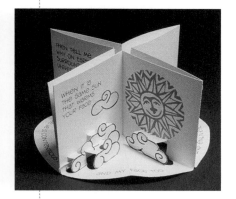

■ CAROUSEL

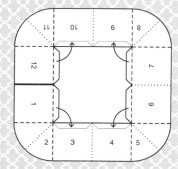

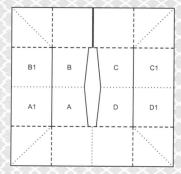

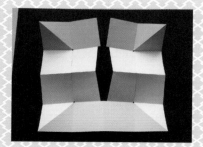

• Another variation is possible by cutting the angles into squares or quarter circles and then gluing the covers at the ends.
Trace the valley folds with a stiletto and slightly mark the mountain folds.
Insert and glue the 1 tabs to the back of page 3 and tab 6 to the back of page 4.
Glue pages 3 and 4 back to back.
The first two quarters of the book are done.
Repeat the operation with the other two quarters. Insert and glue tab 7 to the back of page 9 and tab 12 to the back of page 10.
Glue pages 9 and 10 back to back and then pages 6 and 7 back to back.
To finish, added a cord to pages 1 and 12 to be able to keep the carousel open.

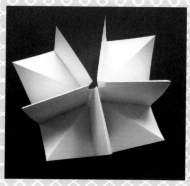

• This model, made with a single sheet, requires special handling. A little folding trick helps give form to a carousel with four foldable scenes. Concept by J.-Ch. Trebbi, 2018.

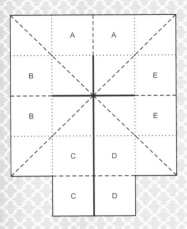

• Serious Stuf, *Ed Hutchins, 1993.*

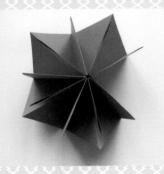

• Petal book, *Ed Hutchins, 1993.*
This model requires two central diagonal cuts;
just a few folds are enough to create this
original carousel. Simple and efficient model that
can be created with children.

"Folding is an invitation to magic. We enter a book through a fold; without it there is no way in or out."
Paul Johnson

Pop-up house, *Paul Johnson, 1998.*

The creation of a simple mini book from a single sheet of folded paper has different names. The generic term, of Anglo-Saxon origin, is booklet. However, other names exist such as chapbook, which comes from the English "chapmen", a word that designates traveling salesmen who in the 16th and 17th centuries, sold a variety of goods, including small cheap books printed on low-quality paper, religious and political tracts, children's songs, poetry and almanacs aimed at spreading popular culture among the general public.

Today, other names such as mini zine, pocket book, and one-page fold book compass the notion of Do It Yourself applied to mini books.

The creation of these books provides a genuine pedagogical opportunity and is the focus of many children's workshops.

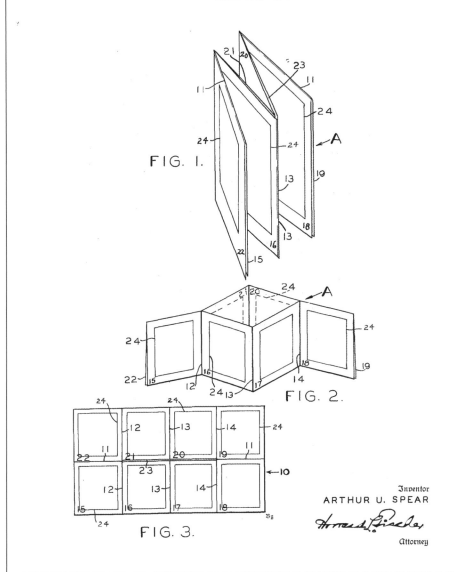

• Patent Arthur U. Spear, 1952.
In 1952, Arthur U. Spear (St. Paul, Minnesota), registered a patent (US. 2,725,651) titled Greeting fold display. It is a card model made with a single sheet of rectangular paper folded in two lengthwise, folded in two again widthways, and folded in two once more to obtain eight identical elements. A longitudinal slit in two sections enables folding the card like a little book. It is the most commonly used base model for making a do-it-yourself mini book.

■ SPEAR PATENT

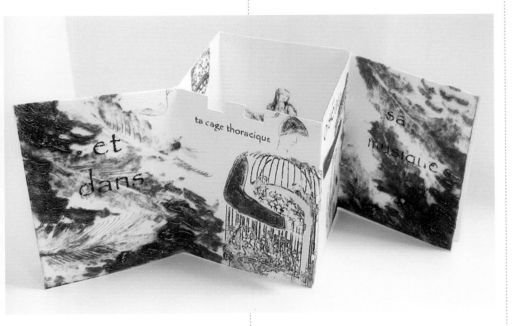

• Pour un oiseau rare,
Frédérique Le Lous Delpech, 2008.
Format: folded, 10 x 15 cm (4 x 6 in);
unfolded, 30 x 40 cm (12 x 16 in).
Technique: engraved in Plexiglass®,
text by Marie-Noëlle Gaillet.

• Green, *Frédérique Le Lous Delpech, 2008.*
Format: folded, 25 x 15 cm (4 x 6 in); unfolded, 60 x 50
cm (12 x 16 in).
Engraved in Plexiglass® and gouache highlighted
collograph, Green text, by Paul Verlaine.

Paul Johnson

GREAT BRITAIN

Paul Johnson is known throughout the world as a pioneer in the development of literacy through the art of the book. He has created books with millions of children worldwide. He is the author of more than fifteen books, the most recent being *New Pop-up Paper Projects* (Routledge, 2013). His pop-up carousel books are included in many collections, among them the Library of Congress in Washington and the Bodleian Library in Oxford.
In 2017, the BBC made a film about him and in 2018, Johns Hopkins University acquired his archives, which contain more than five hundred original elements from his oeuvre created over the course of more than half a century.

"The discovery of the six-page origami book in 1987 changed my life. Later, I found two hundred book projects based on paper and scissors. The book form teaches children to organize their thoughts, arrange their reflections and think sequentially, like when you write a story. A page is not merely a blank sheet of paper but an invisible structure that is the gateway to understanding, expression and communication.

A book is not only a depository of words. It is a well-oiled machine. Creating a book opens up a world of infinite possibilities to us - stories, historical inquiries, geographic explorations... - so that we can arrange our ideas, give them structure and substance, and lead to an encounter with our readers."
Paul Johnson, 2019. Extract from Literacy through the Book Arts.

✎ www.bookart.co.uk/index.html

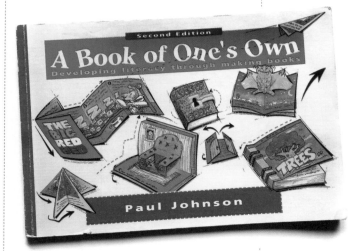

• Pop-up house, *1998*.

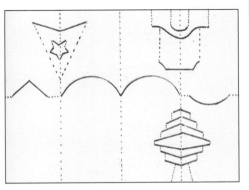

• Silently, the Earth's Heart Watches, 1998.
Format: 9 x 10 x 6 cm (3.5 x 4 x 2 in), 90°
pop-up book, *folded and cut diagram*.

In his work *Literacy through the Book Arts*, Paul Johnson explores the psychology of the fold and the concept of *continuum origami*. In the book, he shares his teaching adventures and describes his educational experiences through his *one sketch books*. These little books are an ideal support that enables children to make books in which they invent stories, often based on their personal experiences.

It is amazing how such a simple structure as a folded sheet of paper with a central cut allows children between 8 and 10 ten years old to discover what a book is and how one is made. With the introduction to basic pop-up book techniques, they learn the recto and verso and develop spatial location with the help of cuts and perforations.

The concertina and structures associated with origami offer surprising opportunities to imagine unexpected forms. The doors, windows and pop-ups renew the conventional image of the page and transform the book into a genuine architecture.

As Paul Johnson states: "Who can resist opening doors and windows and seeing what's on the other side?"

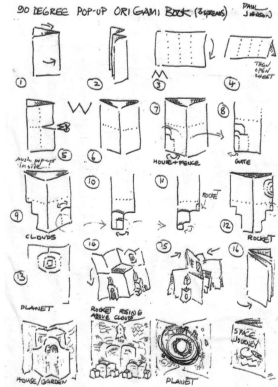

• The Rocket takes off, *sketch by Paul Johnson, 2007. Unfolded format: 15 x 10 x 8 cm (9 x 12 x 3 in).*

• The 3 little pigs house, 2007.
Unfolded format: 21 x 29.7 cm (4 x 0.8 in). According to the two types of cut, a portrait, landscape or Italian format book is obtained. In addition, starting with a square, a vertical rectangle is obtained that, completed with central cuts, adapts better to architectural forms such as houses and castles.
Children are fascinated by striking forms that the center cut produces instead of the shapes of a conventionally folded rectangular book.

Carolyn Leigh
UNITED STATES

Carolyn Leigh is a traveler, painter and artist based in Tucson, Arizona.

Her creations are very colorful and include unique cuts that transform simple books into paper sculptures that play with the form of the central slit.

'Tips for making a four-page origami book: Fold a paper rectangle in eight sections (one time lengthwise and three times widthways). Press the front folds back several times. Fold the paper in two lengthwise. Cut or tear two sections of the fold along the center or cut the unfolded paper with a blade.

Fold in two lengthwise bringing the upper border toward the lower one. Maintain the left and right borders.

Push toward the center so that the two panels are separated and form a cross. Flatten each page and then fold the rectangle in two to make the book.

In addition to a straight cut, many other kinds of cuts can be made in the center. In the example, there is a cut of two buildings with a pointed roof.

The cut in three sections creates an interesting sculpture book. The sections should be examined to ensure they are strong enough when the book is extended. It is also possible to incline the horizontal fold and make vertical folds at unequal intervals.'

Carolyn Leigh, 2008.

✎ www.carolynleigh.com

• Blue Village, *2008.*
"A city cut in three sections with pointed roofs, collection of the Zukoski family. A mini book made with mixed techniques: oil pastels, watercolor, gouache, Pitt markers. Unique copies."

• Santa Monica, *2008.*
"Variation used inside a booklet.
In Santa Monica, the panel of the freeway/ interior play unifies the space and contrasts with the scenes of peaceful strolls along the beach on the outside. In the scene on the beach, a cutout window serves to reveal more of the interior content of the book. I use this format as a back to back to compare and create contrast."

Mini-book, a useful teaching tool

"All you have to do is fold a sheet of paper to make a book from a single piece. You can draw and write stories, print and share... Anybody can be a writer (and publisher) of actual books. As a fledgling school teacher, I was seduced by the teaching possibilities of a tool that, clearly, can become a pretext for working with students on writing, for studying the concept of a book; that can become an opportunity to be introduced to and explore writing, composition, and using a computer. Mini-books are a motivating medium and particularly suitable as a book object for engendering and valuing writing."
Loig Legrand-Lafoy, teacher, extract from Petits livres, un outil au service des apprentissages, *report of the IUFM, Brittany, Vannes region, 2008/2009.*

✎ petitslivres.free.fr/techniques/dossierpro01.pdf

Les Éditions Célestines provides logistical support to writing activities developed in schools, introducing techniques for the creation of mini-books and encouraging the spread of writing produced by students.

✎ petitslivres.free.fr

• *Mini-books made in schools: Brassens preschool, Cléguer; public school in Boismont; Netter preschool, Paris.*

Mini stories

"Children, we have the pleasure of discovering mini stories in the magazine *Spirou,* published by Dupuis, the first publisher, as far as I know, that included in the center of an issue a mini book to be assembled, in the 1960s. Mini stories with tales of Boule et Bill, Bobo, the Schtroumpfs and Gaston, to mention just a few, were published from 1959 to 1995.

After reading the magazine, to find the new story, you had to open the magazine at the middle, take out the staples and carefully remove the two central double pages, fold them following the instructions and cut the pages to obtain a thirty-six page 7 × 10 cm (2.7 × 3.9 in) mini book. To bind it, one or two staples or a small rubber band were added. Beautiful *mise-en-void*! The prolonged reading, and the feeling of having participated in the publication of the magazine, was incredible.

It might seem humdrum, but a book was an object that had something sacred about it, and that gave us the right to alter the magazine and physically appropriate the book.

Later, the Caltec company (General Petroleum Union) also published mini stories as a gift for filling your tank at their service stations. I would beg my father to stop at them!

Other companies, like Mokalux coffee and Entremont cheese, also gave away mini stories."

J.-Ch. Trebbi

📖 www.bdoubliees.com/minirecit/minifab.htm

📖 bdoubliees.com/minirecit/index.html#histo

📖 bachybouzouk.free.fr/souvenirs/collection/caltex_01.html

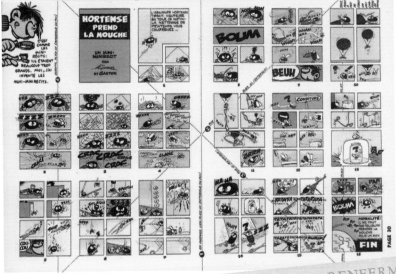

• Gaston, Hortense prend la mouche, Journal de Spirou no.1159, June 30, 1960.

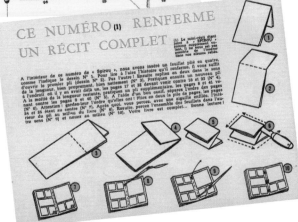

• Journal de Spirou no.1130, January 7, 1960.

• L'œuf et les Schtroumpfs, Journal de Spirou no.1147, April 7, 1960.

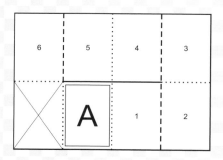

• *Proposal and cut concept for booklet Creation of J.-Ch. Trebbi*

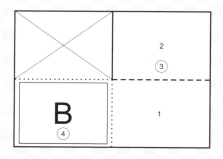

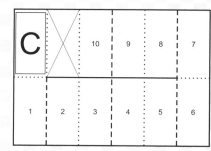

■ MINI BOOKS A - Z

• *This alphabet summary is an overview of the making of twenty-six models of books without binding between 4 and 30 pages.*
These preparation diagrams include folds, cuts and incisions in the center or around the sheet.

The mini books are made from a sheet of standardized A4 (a sheet of U.S. letter size) (21 x 29.7 cm) (8 x12 in) paper, but for mini books with a lot of pages it is preferable to use lightweight A3 (tabloid) (29.7 x 42 cm) (12 x 17 in) format paper.

Modifying the position of the cuts results in new folds. The inclusion of oblique folds allows for changing the mini book's general shape.

• *Number of pages obtained according to the references in the models:*

4 pages: A; Y.	18 pages: J; O.
6 pages: B; E.	20 pages: H.
8 pages: N; P; R.	22 pages: G; W.
10 pages: C; F; M.	26 pages: Z.
12 pages: L; V; X.	30 pages: K; T.
14 pages: D; I; Q; S; U.	

• *Graphic representation of the folds.*

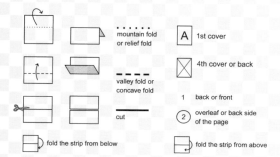

⋯⋯	mountain fold or relief fold
– – –	valley fold or concave fold
——	cut
🔪	fold the strip from below

A	1st cover
⊠	4th cover or back
1	back or front
②	overleaf or back side of the page
	fold the strip from above

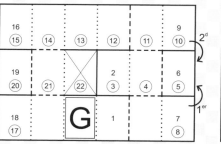

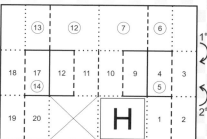

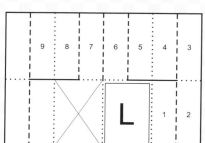

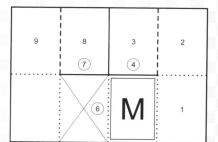

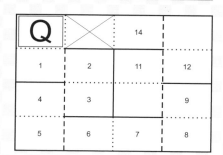

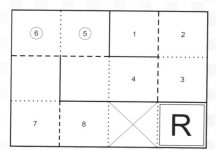

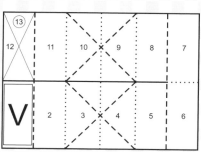

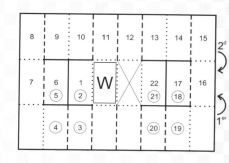

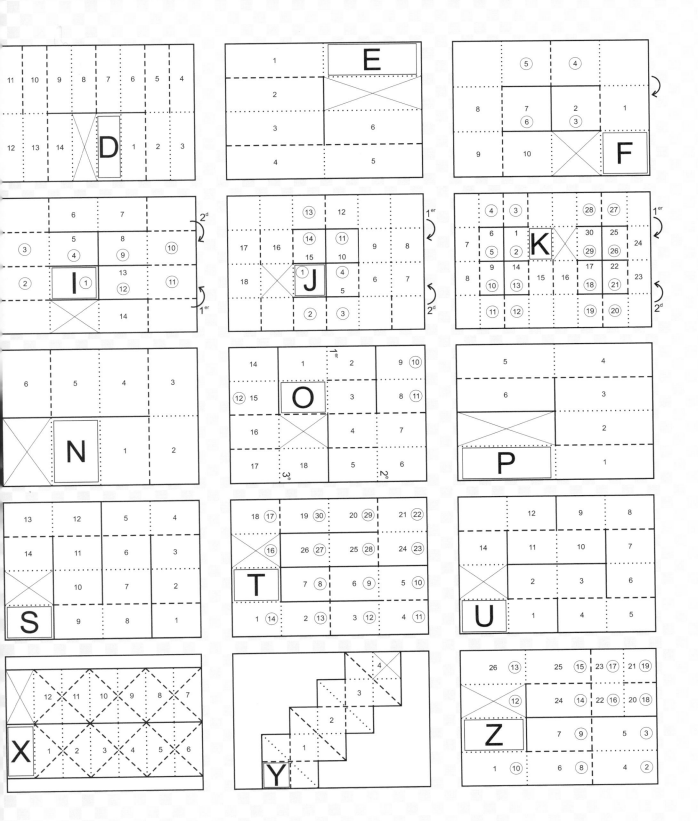

Papers and folds

Origami papers and Japan papers

"In the choice of papers three criteria are at play: thickness, texture and color. The classic origami paper is superfine. A wide range of colors appears on one side, while the other is white, making the diagrams of the books easier to follow. Some origami papers have texture. Others are iridescent to play with light or have patterns and are more suitable for making boxes and characters. Sometimes it is good to use a two-tone superfine origami paper, with a different color on each side, and even at times in a degraded color.

Kraft paper, for instance, is highly resistant and is ideal for everyday folds.

Washi is a fine, flexible yet solid paper that has been produced in Japan for 1300 years and is often used in origami. *Washi* is the generic term used to refer to paper manufactured in Japan. The term is made up of *wa* ("Japanese") and *shi* ("paper").

Tant paper is the king of origami papers: fine and easy to fold. It is one of the most multifaceted origami papers. It is suitable for both simple and complex models, as well as modular, tessellated and folded models of all kinds of animals and characters. It is age-resistant and neither fades nor deteriorates. The normal sizes have a square format: 15 ×15 cm (6 × 6 in) or 20 × 20 cm (8 × 8 in). For mini folds there are 7.5 ×7.5 cm (3 × 3 in), and *35 x 35 cm (14 x 14 in)* in elephant paper."
Nicolas Terry, January 2020.

✎ www.origami-shop.com

✎ www.happyfolding.com/paper-review_tant

Weight, pH and direction of the paper

The weight defines the mass of the paper per surface unit. The lower it is (between 80 and 170 g/m²) (30 and 63 lb), the softer the paper, while a high weight (between 350 y 400 g/m²) (129 and 148 lb) corresponds to a rigid paper.

The pH ("potential of hydrogen") is the unit of measure of the degree of acidity from 0 to 14. A neutral or base (non-acid) paper is paper with a pH between 6 and 7. Its acidity is ideal and guarantees good preservation over time; but it could still contain impurities that would make it more fragile. A pH of 1 corresponds to higher acidity.

Paper pulp is made up of fibers. Depending on the manufacturing method, the directions of handmade papers or paper produced in a mold are not differentiated. But industrial paper has two directions: the machine direction (longitudinal) and the cross section, and the sheet of paper must be used in one direction or the other according to the needs.
In folding and binding jobs, the sheet is more easily folded longitudinally.
In contrast, in the preparation of pop-up cards, the central fold, in which the opening and the closing of the sheet are made, must be perpendicular to the direction of the fibers. It is necessary to mark the folds beforehand with a stiletto, to compress the fibers topically.
Yet if couché paper is used, which is covered with several layers of pigments and binding agents that harden its surface, directions will not present a problem.
To determine the direction of the paper, two strips of the same size are cut in the two directions of the paper. The one that folds more when it is taken by the ends is the one that has been cut crosswise.

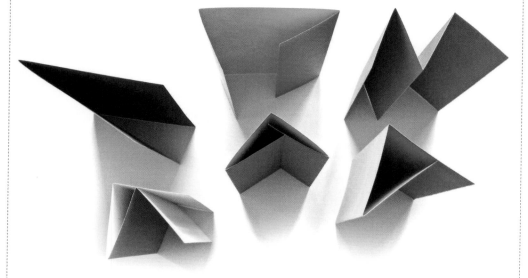

Mini book made from recovered papers.
Creation of D. Couchaux.

⇨ www.lateliercanson.com/choisir-son-materiel-de-conservation

⇨ www.lesgrandesimprimeries.com/calculer-le-poids-papier-feuille-documents

⇨ glossairedupapetier.fr/s.html

Booklet folds

To ensure the folds are made correctly, it is a good idea to keep in mind the dimensions of the sheets once they are folded with a tolerance backlash. As a result, some parts will be slightly shorter. For example, for an accordion fold from three sheets of paper, the sheets will have the same dimensions since they overlap, while in a fold consisting of two encircling folds with three parts on a A4 sheet (210 x 297 mm) (8.2 x 11.6 in) base, the first two parts will be 100 mm (3.8 in) long and the last will be narrower (97 mm) (3.9 in).

⇨ www.imprimini.fr/wp-content/uploads/2017/02/Guide-PAO-technique-IMPRIMINI.pdf

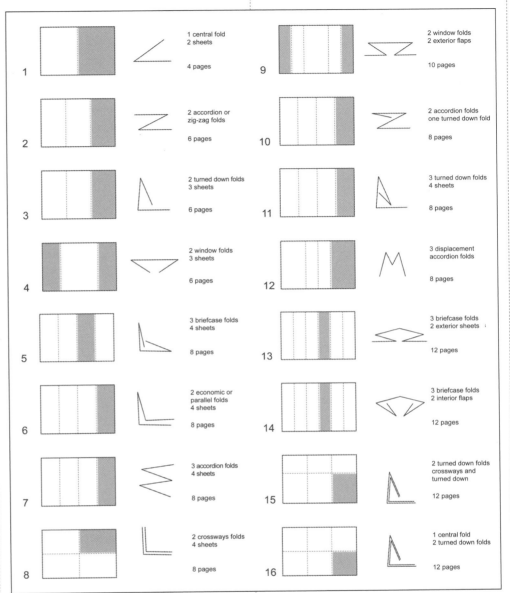

• Beginning of the folding of sheets of paper and types of folds.

Central fold: the sheet is folded simply in 2.

Accordion fold or Z-fold: fold resulting from several parallel folds following the shape of an accordion or a zig-zag pattern.

Encircling fold: parallel folds that enable overlapping the different parts obtained in this way and closing the document on itself; up to five parts can be folded like a spiral.

Window fold: parallel fold consisting of two folds; the two parts are folded toward the center of the sheet of paper.

Wallet fold: fold made up of three parallel folds that enables folding two exterior sheets toward the interior central fold.

Economic fold: the sheet of paper is folded in two and then folded onto itself in a fold parallel to the previous ones. This allows for an eight-page fold-away object without cuts or staples.

Cross fold: fold resulting from several folds perpendicular to each other.

Bibliography

ASUNCION Josep, *Le papier, création et fabrication,* ed. Gründ, 2002.

CHATANI Masahiro, *Origamic Architecture of Masahiro Chatani*, Shokokusha, Tokyo, 1983.

DELPUECH Yves, *Le Papier, Les hauts lieux des arts graphiques*, self-published, Montigny-le-Bretonneux, 2010.

DENIS Guillaume, *Origami, vol. 1, les bases,* published by Eyrolles, Paris, 2018.

DUPUIGRENET-DESROUSSILLES François, "La galaxie Tsaï-Loun", *Les Cahiers de médiologie*, 1997/2 (no. 4), p. 65-83.

GAUTIER Martine, *Murmures de papier*, self-published, Saint-Nazaire, 2018.

GONSE François, *Les papiers japonais, traditions et créations,* published by Ouest France, 2004.

GRAND-CARTERET John, *Vieux papiers, vieilles images,* published by A. Le Vasseur & Cie, Paris, 1896.

HUTCHINS Edward, *Book dynamics!,* Editions, 2009.

JOHNSON Paul, *Pop-up paper engineering,* The Falmer Press, London, 1992.

JOHNSON Paul, *Literacy Through the Book Arts,* Heinemann, Portsmouth, 1993.

JOHNSON Paul, *A Book of One's Own*, Heinemann, Portsmouth, NH, 1998.

KASAHARA Kunihiko, *El Mundo Nuevo*, published by Sanrio, 1989.

KENNEWAY Eric, *Complete origami*, Ebury Press, London, 1987.

PAULAIS Martine, *Papier, créations et métamorphoses*, published by Dessain et Tolra/Larousse, Paris, 2006.

PREVOT Pascal, ROCHER Fabien, *Techniques d'impression, Cours d'industries graphiques*, published by Eyrolles, Paris, 2006.

RUTZKY Jeffrey, *Kirigami, exquisite projects to fold and cut*, Barnes & Nobles, New York, 2007.

TREBBI Jean-Charles, *The Art of Folding,* Promopress, Hoaki Books, Barcelona 2012.

TREBBI Jean-Charles, *The Art of Cutting,* Promopress, Hoaki Books, Barcelona, 2015.

TREBBI Jean-Charles, *The Art of Pop-Up,* Promopress, Hoaki Books, Barcelona, 2012.

TREBBI J-Ch., BOUNOURE G., GENEVAUX C., *The Art of Folding vol. 2*, Promopress, Hoaki Books, Barcelona, 2017.

TREBBI Jean-Charles, *Basic Pop-Up*, published by Eyrolles, Paris, 2016.

VERNUS Michel, *La fabuleuse histoire du papier,* published by Cabédita, 2004.

Fold

A mini book that features the collection of works devoted to the fold and the cut by Jean-Charles Trebbi.

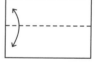

Acknowledgments

Heartfelt thanks to all the artists, creators, photographers and contributors for enthusiastically agreeing to participate in this new publishing adventure:
Miyako Akai - Hélène Baumel y Ross Gash - Diana Bloomfield - Laurence Bucourt - Patricia Cavrois - Nicolas Codron - Béatrice Coron y Étienne Frossard - Annwyn Dean - Isabelle Faivre - Martine Gautier, Emile Goozairow - Peter D. Gerakaris - Jeroen Hillhorst - Emmanuelle Jamme - Jacques Desse - Paul Johnson - Hedi Kyle - Ulla and Paul Warchol - Frédérique Le Lous Delpech - Julie Auzillon - Jean-Jacques Delalandre - Carolyn Leigh - Kenneth Leslie - Kristine Suhr - Eni Looka - Marjon Mudde - Philippe Morlot - Elsa Mroziewicz - Gisela Oberbeck y Christoph Knoch - Catherine y Kimihito Okuyama - Thomas Parker Williams - Laurent Husson - Malica Lestang - Philippe Phérivong - Gina Pisello - Jean-Claude Planchenault - Kelly Seojung Lee - Shirley Sharoff - Kevin Steele - Lisa Giles - Annette Mauer y Melissa Silk - Nicolas Terry - Coco Téxèdre and Arnaud Schultz - and *Special Warm Thanks* to Ed Hutchins for his documentary assistance and sage advice.

My deepest thanks for sharing their knowledge, their wide-ranging creative searches, publication permission and friendly expressions of kindness:
Patrice Aoust y Gérard Aimé - Marie-Christine Guyonnet, La Librairie du Ciel - Chantal and Paul Leibenguth, Am'Arts - Thibaut Brunessaux, La Boutique du Livre animé et Les Libraires associés - Hélène Valotteau y Christelle Moreau, mediateca Françoise Sagan/ Fonds Patrimonial Jeunesse Heure Joyeuse - Pietro Franchi - Agnès Breuillaud - Yves Delpuech

Brigitte Merlin - Sophie Giraud y Rozenn Samson, Hélium Éditions - Clementine Sourdais - Lindsay Ellinas, Vamp & Tramp Booksellers, LLC - Jean Poderos and Laurine Bougis, Éditions Courtes et Longues - Loïc Maiche y Adrien Bigey, ADM impression - Gaby y Christiane Lemaire - Patrick Bertholon y los Fujak - Margrit Neuendorf and Olivier Huet - Benjamin Lacour, Escuela elemental Federico Garcia Lorca, Vaulx-en-Velin - Les Éditions Célestines - Loig and Émilie Legrand-Lafoy; to the members of the M.F.P.P, enthusiastic and creative folders and in particular to Claudine Pisasale - Yves Clavel - Alain Joisel - Guillaume Denis - François Dulac - Raymonde Bonnefille - Michel Grand - Barth Duncan.

Special thanks:
to Nicole and Denis, for their creative ideas and suggestions;
to my editors, Charlotte Gallimard and Sabine Bledniak for their trust;
to Cécile Lebreton, for the care shown in the production of this book;
to Sophie Gallet, Hélène Clastres, Mathilde Barrois, Coline Briand and Camille Dejardin for their professionalism;
to Denis Couchaux, for his always highly insightful layout ideas, his friendly cooperation and his artistic involvement in this new work.

• *Isabelle Faivre, see p. 17.*

• *Isabelle Faivre, see p. 17.*

• Le Petit Chaperon rouge, *Clémentine Sourdais, Hélium publishing, 2013.*

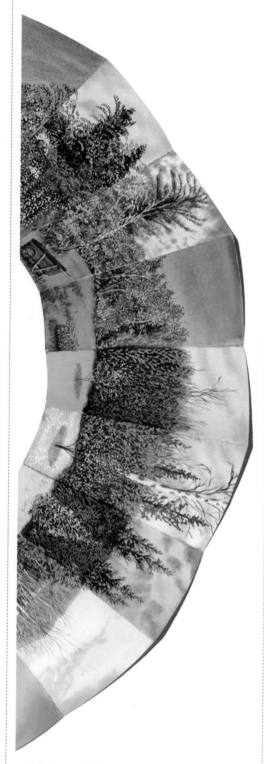

• Ken Leslie, see p. 126.

Photography credits

P. 4 tl: Coco Téxèdre; p. 4 cl: Laurence Bucourt; p. 4 bl: Kevin Steele; p. 5 tl: Hedi Kyle; p. 5 bl: Paul Johnson; p. 7: Gina Pisello, p. 8: Arnaud Schultz, p. 10 tl: Peter D.Gerakaris, p. 10 bl: Isabelle Faivre, p. 11 tr: Miyako Akai, p. 11 br: Arnaud Schultz, p. 12 bl: Frédérique Le Lous Delpech, p. 16: Arnaud Schultz, p. 17: Ross Gash, p. 18 tl: Malica Lestang, p. 18 br: Marjon Mudde, p. 19 cl, bl: Isabelle Faivre, p. 19 br: Emile Goozairow, p. 20: Miyako Akai, p. 21: Emile Goozairow, p. 22, p. 23: Gina Pisello, p. 24 bl and br: Emile Goozairow, p. 25 tr and br: Eni Looka; p. 26, p. 27: Steampop and Lisa Giles; p. 29, p. 30, p.31 tr: Jean-Jacques Delalandre; p.32 Peter D.Gerakaris; p. 35: Annwyn Dean; p. 39: Laurence Bucourt; p. 40, p. 41: Kevin Steele; p. 42, p. 43: Diana Bloomfield; p. 44, p. 45: Peter D.Gerakaris; p.47, p. 48, p. 49: Gina Pisello; p. 54, p. 55, p. 56: Edward H. Hutchins; p. 64: Frédérique Le Lous Delpech; p. 66 br: Annwyn Dean; p. 67: Kevin Steele; p. 68: Laurence Bucourt; p. 69: Gina Pisello; p. 70 bl: Arnaud Schultz; p. 71: Miyako Akai; p. 72, p. 73: Emile Goozairow; p. 78: Jean-Claude Planchenault; p. 82 br, p. 83: Edward H. Hutchins; p. 84, p. 85: Christoph Knoch; p. 86, p. 87: Etienne Frossard; p. 96: Nicolas Codron; p. 98: Laurent Husson; p. 99: Isabelle Faivre; p. 100, p. 101: Catherine Okuyama; p. 102: Frédérique Le Lous Delpech; p. 103: Elsa Mroziewicz; p. 105: Emmanuelle Jamme; p. 106: Kevin Steele; p. 107: Laurence Bucourt; p. 108: Annwyn Dean; p. 109: Gina Pisello; p. 110, p. 111, p. 112: Ulla y Paul Warchol; p. 116: Emile Goozairow; p. 118 tr: Eni Looka; p. 118 br: Frédérique Le Lous Delpech; p. 119: Shirley voir nom photograph; p. 120, p. 121: Philippe Morlot; p. 122: Kelly Seojung Lee; p. 123 tr: Philippe Morlot; p. 123 br: Kenneth Leslie; p. 124: Martine Gautier; p. 125 tr: Isabelle Faivre; p. 126: Thomas Parker Williams; p. 127 tl, cl, bl: Edward H. Hutchins; p. 128, p. 129: Kenneth Leslie; p. 130 tl and tr: Thomas Parker Williams; p. 130 br: Philippe Morlot; p. 132, p. 133: Kevin Steele; p. 134, p. 135, p. 136: Edward H. Hutchins; p. 141 ai: Etienne Frossard; p. 142, p. 143 tl, tr: Edward H. Hutchins; p. 143 bl, br: Kristine Suhr; p. 144 tr: Edward H. Hutchins; p. 144 cl: Kristine Suhr; p. 145 br: Patricia Cavrois; p. 150, p. 151, p. 157 br; p. 159: Edward H. Hutchins; p. 160: Paul Johnson; p. 163: Frédérique Le Lous Delpech; p. 164, p. 165, p. 166: Paul Johnson, p. 167: Carolyn Leigh; p. 168: Loig Legrand-Lafoy; p. 173: Denis Couchaux; p. 177 b: Clémentine Sourdais; p. 177 r: Isabelle Faivre; p. 178: Ken Leslie; 4th cover: Gina Pisello.

Diagrams computer graphics: Denis Trebbi.

Uncredited photographs and sketches are the author's.
Unfortunately, we were unable to identify certain photographs. We promise to make the necessary changes after authenticating these images.